THE
TERRORIST
FACTORY

Also by Father Patrick Desbois

In Broad Daylight:
The Secret Procedures behind the Holocaust by Bullets

THE
TERRORIST
FACTORY

ISIS, THE YAZIDI GENOCIDE, AND EXPORTING TERROR

FATHER PATRICK DESBOIS

AND

COSTEL NASTASIE

WITH A FOREWORD BY LARA LOGAN

TRANSLATED FROM THE FRENCH BY
SHELLEY TEMCHIN

Arcade Publishing • New York

First English-language Edition

Originally published in French under the title *La Fabrique des terroristes* by Librairie
Arthème Fayard

Arcade Publishing books may be purchased in bulk at special discounts for
sales promotion, corporate gifts, fund-raising, or educational purposes. Special
editions can also be created to specifications. For details, contact the Special Sales
Department, Arcade Publishing, 307 West 36th Street, 11th Floor, New York,
NY 10018 or arcade@skyhorsepublishing.com.

Arcade Publishing® is a registered trademark of Skyhorse Publishing, Inc.®,
a Delaware corporation.

Visit our website at www.arcadepub.com.
Visit the authors' sites at www.yahadinunum.org and romadignity.org.

10 9 8 7 6 5 4 3 2 1

Library of Congress Cataloging-in-Publication Data

Names: Desbois, Patrick, author. | Nastasie, Costel, author. | Temchin,
  Shelley, translator.
Title: The terrorist factory: ISIS, the Yazidi genocide, and exporting
  terror / Father Patrick Desbois and Costel Nastasie ; translated from the
  French by Shelley Temchin ; foreword by Lara Logan.
Other titles: Fabrique des terroristes. English
Description: New York, NY: Arcade Publishing, 2018.
Identifiers: LCCN 2018008917 (print) | LCCN 2018013254 (ebook) | ISBN
  9781628729481 (ebook) | ISBN 9781628729467 | ISBN
  9781628729467(hardcover:alk. paper) | ISBN 9781628729481(ebook)
Subjects: LCSH: IS (Organization) | Yezidis—Iraq—History—21st century. |
  Genocide—Iraq—History—21st century.
Classification: LCC HV6433.I722 (ebook) | LCC HV6433.I722 D4713 2018 (print)
  | DDC 363.32509567—dc23
LC record available at https://lccn.loc.gov/2018008917

Cover design by Erin Seaward-Hiatt
Cover photograph: Yahad-In Unum

Printed in the United States of America

CONTENTS

FOREWORD

This book was not built on anonymous sources, or on second-hand accounts or political narratives. It is the simple, honest product of thousands of hours of hard work, precise investigative techniques, and a pure commitment to understanding and knowing the truth. I cannot think of anyone more qualified than Father Patrick Desbois to take us inside the machinery of genocide and terror that has defined ISIS since they first struck fear in our hearts.

He brings to this task not only his knowledge and experience, but his understanding of the innate capacity to kill that informs us all. He did not come by this knowledge easily. Father Desbois has spent much of his life studying this particular aspect of the human condition—not from a distance, but always in person.

Year after year, he has walked in the footsteps of terrorists and murderers, from the remote villages of Eastern Europe to dusty villages in Guatemala to ancient towns across northern Iraq. And he does not go alone. Together with his chief investigator, Costel Nastasie, at his side, they are a formidable pair. I know of no equal.

They never forget a detail, or a face, always coming back to question, to learn, to discover, to confirm or reject. Perhaps most importantly, they come without ego and without agenda. Over countless hours of recorded interviews and many more informal meetings and conversations, they ask the most simple, straightforward questions. They do not judge, they do not lead. And that is what makes this book so powerful. There is only one truth, and truth is their only master.

They are not seeking to serve the interests of any one of us, just the interests of us all. For if we cannot understand and know what we face, how can we possibly overcome?

It is a mystery to me that they stand alone in the work they have done. I have not encountered anywhere else the details, the insight, and the evidence they report in these pages. How can something of such significance rest in such a profound way on the shoulders of a Catholic priest and a Roma? Who ask for nothing but our attention and our conscience? Whose only motivation is to document, for all of us, exactly what we face today, so that we cannot claim falsely years later—as others have done before us—that "we did not know."

What makes this book so memorable is not just the details, it is the humanity with which they were gathered and with which they are told. No matter how difficult the terrain, no matter how weary or frustrated or defeated they may have been along the way, the authors never abandoned their humanity or their integrity. And they never stopped or doubted—not even for a moment.

The insight Father Patrick Desbois and Costel Nastasie have given us is terrifying.

And it should not end here.

LARA LOGAN
60 MINUTES

PREFACE
TO THE ENGLISH-LANGUAGE EDITION

This book was written more than a year ago. ISIS was the absolute ruler over large swaths of Syria and Iraq, with Raqqa and Mosul as its capitals. At the time, we were interviewing Yazidis who had recently escaped the clutches of the Islamic State, which viewed this Mesopotamian people as *kuffar*, infidels, and therefore fair game for all manner of crimes. In their captors' murderous ideology, the wholesale rape, torture, and murder that the Yazidis endured was justified.

We thought then that the defeat of ISIS would mean freedom for all of its slaves. It hasn't turned out that way.

Today, in 2018, the war appears to be over. The international press and world leaders have declared ISIS to be dead or dying: Iraq and Syria seem to have emerged from the shadow of its dark flag. Some say its leader, Abu Bakr al-Baghdadi, has been killed by Russian bombs; others claim that he is alive but injured, and under medical care in Libya. Little by little, public opinion in democratic countries has forgotten the shootings, bombings, beheadings, crucifixions, and black flags of an empire that seems to have crumbled. Aren't mass amnesia and individual forgetfulness the necessary price of a comfortable life and untroubled sleep?

What I find most surprising in Iraq in this month of March 2018 is the freed Yazidi children, young girls and boys, who are returning, little by little every day, every week, to displaced-persons camps to be reunited with their families. But what are they returning from? ISIS has been declared dead, but its members are still alive, and its slaves are still in their grip. Are they hidden in refugee camps, or have they melted away, unnoticed, into the crowds of people? Have they left for Libya, the Sahel, the Sinai, or Afghanistan? Or Europe?

Yet, if ISIS surely lost many battles, there is one war it seems to have won: with its child-terrorist factories.

Indeed, a number of recently-freed Yazidi boys and girls continue to tell us not only about beatings and training camps but also about their own participation in the fighting and the murder of civilians. These children were transformed into actual or potential killers in the name of the ISIS caliphate. They may have been rescued from hell, but often they have forgotten their native language and sometimes even the faces of their parents. Today, they speak the language of the people who bought them, Arabic or Turkish but also English. This morning, here in Iraq, not far from Dohuk, a nine-year-old boy was telling us in perfect English that he is American, not Yazidi. Indeed, his uncle, sitting next to him, says the child was bought by an American ISIS family in Syria. He no longer understands a word of Kurdish. In his mind and memory, he is a member of ISIS—an American member of ISIS.

It's as if these children, these "ghosts of the Islamic state," have been stripped of their identity. If their bodies seem to have survived hell, their identity has not. They have lost their names, their religion, their language, and even the memory of their mothers and fathers. These "lion cubs of the caliphate" have learned how to commit murder or die in order to kill. Many of them remain in contact with members of ISIS via social media. They dream of nothing but combat and heroic vengeance.

The adults, the older members of ISIS, in fact told them, "We grown-ups, men and women of the Islamic State, will all die in Raqqa or in Mosul, but you youngsters, you lion cubs, will live."

Today, these children are returning as best they can to their native land, with or without their parents. Will they forget the delayed-action mission to kill that was conferred on them? Will they forget the responsibility that ISIS has handed down to them post-mortem?

One of them, an eleven-year-old, looked us straight in the eye and said, "I will form a special forces unit of ISIS right here."

In their eyes, the Islamic State is not dead. They were, they are, they perhaps will be the ISIS heroes of tomorrow.

Our democracies are ill-equipped to deal with these young people, not child soldiers but child terrorists who for more than three years have been spilling out from the ranks of the Islamic State.

ISIS: the maker and exporter of child terrorists.

NEAR DOHUK, IRAQI KURDISTAN
MARCH 2018

THE

TERRORIST
FACTORY

TAKING UP MY PEN

July 24, 2014—New York
1777 Avenue of the Americas

It feels like we aren't moving at all. There isn't even that knot in the pit of your stomach, the kind you have when you're jolted by an unexpected movement. Still, the little numbers on the screen are whizzing upward. No doubt about it—we are rising. The elevator is silently chewing up the floors.

I quickly look around the cabin: gold walls and a large mirror that makes me look washed out in the harsh light. With a barely noticeable jolt, the elevator stops. The number "40," blue against the black background of the panel, flashes. The sliding doors open with a *whoosh*.

Behind a brown counter, a smartly dressed young woman, appearing refined and serious, greets us with, "How can I help you?"

I identify myself: "I'm Father Desbois." So does my companion, Robin, the United States representative of Yahad-In

Unum. With her big bag slung across her chest and her hair pinned back, she looks out of place amid all this elegance, but she declares confidently, "We have an appointment with Mr. Howard."

The receptionist nods, picks up her phone, and says a few words before getting up and inviting us to follow her into the conference room. She steps aside to let us enter. Large, comfortable black armchairs surround a massive glass-topped table.

"Would you like something to drink?" she asks.

"We wouldn't turn down some cold water if you have any. Thank you very much."

She disappears for a few moments. The two little clear plastic bottles are damp and leave wet circles on the table.

I have barely taken a few sips when Mr. Howard enters. He is tall and self-assured, with a steady smile that softens his determined look. He comes over and greets us.

I spend the next hour laying out in detail the work we've been doing through Yahad-In Unum. Since 2004, we have been scouring Eastern Europe in search of mass graves of Jews and Roma, victims of the Holocaust by bullets. We have been digging up these bodies, this too-long-ignored chapter in history, as a way of paying homage to those victims and preventing future collective massacres. In more than a hundred expeditions, we've been able to conduct more than 4,000 eyewitness interviews and locate about 1,900 execution sites. Our meeting with Mr. Howard is crucial, since he's financing our investigations. He listens carefully, without interrupting, to what I'm saying. His smile has disappeared.

August 11, 2014—Paris

Paris awakens. The heat wave is over. It's early. I switch on my computer, as I do every morning, a ritual I follow even before I turn on the light in the kitchen to pour my first cup of coffee. I drink it the way a smoker inhales his first cigarette: parched, still thirsty after the first gulp, trying to make the moment last. While my computer is booting up and the water is heating in the coffeemaker, I turn on the television to catch up on the news.

For the last few days, men in black have been taking over the screens. Carefully posed bearded faces declare war on the West, which they refer to as "Rome," and Westerners, whom they call "Crusaders." Between two commercials, images of civilians fleeing death flash by. ISIS units, to the astonishment of our part of the world, are gaining ground in both Iraq and Syria. Their founder, one Abu Bakr al-Baghdadi, has proclaimed a so-called caliphate, to which he is seeking to rally all Muslims. In Iraq, on August 3, 2014, they invaded and conquered Sinjar, the historical city of the Yazidis.

Yazidis. I had never heard the word. How cruelly ironic that I should learn of a people's existence at the very moment it risked vanishing.

I hear the familiar little tune that lets me know the computer is ready. I enter the password and check my email. One sender's name catches my attention: Howard. I click, and the words appear: "I have great respect for what Father Desbois is doing to shed light on the past, but I want to support action that will stop the murders occurring now. In the present."

My life has been punctuated by words that, once heard, have rung true, have broken through somehow and changed me. I still remember something Mother Teresa said forty years ago in Calcutta in a conversation around a table: "If God calls you, He will never let you go." In times of doubt, those words stick with me and guide me like a lighthouse beam in the night.

In a fraction of a second, Mr. Howard's words open my eyes and resonate in my spirit like a thunderclap.

While my coffee is cooling in the cup, my eyes move from the computer screen to the television, where, in full view of the world, the men in black are committing mass murder, killing civilians. I have spent hours listening to the news on TV and reading articles without actually seeing this genocide for what it is. I feel as if I've been deaf and blind to the massacres being committed by ISIS. This reality, concealed until now along with my own responsibility, suddenly appears plain as day. Cruel and violent, it is unacceptable.

Mr. Howard's message has opened my eyes and become an obligation, a resolve.

I cannot and will not devote myself solely to the genocides of the past any longer. I want and need to take up my travels and my pen and devote my heart and mind to the Yazidis who are dying now, today, so near us. I know I won't return unscathed, but I must assume that risk, that responsibility. I must get closer.

February 2015—Brussels

The air is cold and damp. Night has fallen. It's late, and I have to catch the last train to Paris. I'm sitting in the car with Valy as he drives me to the station. He's the young man in charge of Yahad-In Unum's research on the genocide of the Roma. His own family was deported to Kovalivka, a village in what is now Ukraine. Many never returned.

I push up the sleeve of my black jacket to check my watch. We have a little time, so I ask him, "I have an official meeting tomorrow morning. Would there be any barbershops open around here?"

Valy's gaze meets mine in the rearview mirror: "Yes, I know of one." The black BMW speeds through the crowded streets of Brussels as quickly as possible. We waste five minutes trying to find a parking spot on Anspach Boulevard. With a routine gesture, I check that the door is locked, pulling on the handle, which doesn't give. Valy leads me to a shop window on the left. On the front, a sign in large letters reads: ORIA HAIR STYLING SALON FOR MEN. We go in.

Inside, there are men circling around other men who are seated in chairs. The floor is strewn with hair. "Any possibility of a trim?" asks Valy. Three faces turn toward us. "A few minutes!" one of them answers, seating me in a bright red leather chair. He's a young man, hair in a Mohawk, dressed in an outfit that can't help but draw my attention: traditional, very Eastern-looking, with a fitted jacket, custom-made, whose exact origin I can't identify. "He doesn't look familiar," whispers Valy, "but I bet he is a Roma."

When the young man comes back to shave me, I take off my round glasses and, intrigued, ask the question that I've asked thousands of times of people from all walks of life: "Where are you from?"

A person's background isn't simply a natural attribute: your culture, your homeland, the place of your birth often determine how you see and understand the world, how you relate to others.

In a quiet voice, the young man tells me, "I'm Iraqi." I'm jolted—internally only, since the razor on my neck keeps me from moving.

Iraq, for me, is a distant land, which I know has been racked by war but which remains only an idea: a country destroyed, a succession of images imprinted on my eyes, far away and unreal, despite my recent resolve to go there. All at once, the young barber concentrating on the task at hand becomes, for me, the embodiment of Iraq.

Astounded, I explain to him, as if to balance things out by providing some information about my own life, that I'm interested in victims of genocide and that I've recently heard about the persecutions inflicted on the Yazidis and Christians. Silence from the young man.

For several minutes, the scraping of the razor and some faint Arab music are the only sounds I hear. Then comes what I term an "encounter."

Still shaping the contours of my beard, the young man whispers in a barely audible murmur, "I'm a Yazidi, but my boss doesn't know it," before returning to silence. Those few words gave me such a shock that I have no memory of the rest of the conversation.

The time has come for me to take responsibility. For more than six months, I've been searching for a way to draw closer to these people I've heard about but have never met. I've been thinking of buying a plane ticket, organizing an expedition, but I've had no intermediary, no bridge . . . but

I've just found one, as night is falling in Brussels, because I decided to get my beard trimmed.

For me, God remains the summons to a meeting that is thrust upon you. The meeting and the power of speech point me toward a place of promises to keep. Seated behind me in a blue armchair, Valy understands what is happening. In his expression, I see surprise and a touch of worry. He whispers, "Should we wait for him?"

At 10:45, the barbershop closes, and we invite the young barber for a drink at a deserted outdoor café. His name is Zaher, and he left Iraq in 2009 to escape the steadily mounting tensions between the Yazidis and their Muslim neighbors. His family, on the other hand, has stayed behind. The family home is in a village near Essian, one of the biggest Yazidi refugee camps.

The young man recounts at length the story of the genocide of his people.

July 29, 2015—Erbil
Iraqi Kurdistan

The Turkish Airlines flight is preparing to land in total darkness on a runway at Erbil airport, in the capital of Iraqi Kurdistan. Finally.

A few hours earlier, we had a long layover in Turkey. Istanbul's immense, colorful airport with its labyrinth of shops and security gates is as busy at night as during the day. The whole team was sitting on the white leatherette chairs of a cafeteria that was still open despite the late hour. I gratefully examined the faces of those who had agreed to brave the dangers of this trip with me.

Oscar, the cameraman from Costa Rica. Victoria, the Guatemalan photographer with whom I had done all my research on the genocide of the Roma. Two of Zaher's cousins, Rebar and Sebar, who are also refugees, had spread open a map of Syria and Iraq. They were pointing out to Valy the major cities of the so-called caliphate. Zaher appeared to be looking on distractedly. For my part, I was staring off into space. I was already en route to Iraq, while thinking back on the months that had just gone by. Setting up a team hadn't been easy, what with the fear elicited by the question "Do you want to come to Iraq with us?"

The time passed slowly. We took no notice of the thousands of boxes of Turkish delight of every kind, neatly displayed to tempt customers. On the opposite side were the luxury products one finds in every airport, glowing under the bright white lights: Cartier, Hugo Boss, Clarins. Brand names guide the traveler through a world of perfume, alcohol, and cigarettes, whose roads and byways are as familiar as those of any city.

On the plane to Erbil, our eyelids were heavy, and we spoke little. There was no need, since we all knew what the others were thinking. We were going to try to preserve the words, faces, gestures, and memories of the Yazidi victims of the genocide orchestrated by ISIS, and we were all conscious of the responsibility weighing on our shoulders. When brotherhood is the act of reaching out toward others, one's existence is put at risk.

For the moment, there are no happy endings, no superheroes to stay the hands of the killers. There are only whispered stories, full of tears and blood, and haggard faces darkened with pain and fear.

As the plane begins its descent, I lean forward to look outside. I am seated on the aisle, which gives me the illusion of being free to move around but prevents me from viewing the ground. I hate feeling cooped up. Through the window there is nothing but the black night, no light. Around me, the faces are weary, some sleepy, every one of them silent. Not even the white hat and apron of one of the stewards, which make the plane seem like an airborne restaurant, are reassuring. Maybe it's because of our destination. We say "Kurdistan" to avoid thinking "Iraq," a land ravaged by war. Some returning to their country wear the dread of a person pushing open the door to his home when there is no prospect of happiness there.

The wheels hit the tarmac, and the plane bounces slightly. I sink back in my seat to cushion the unpleasant sensation of hard braking. The plane stops moving, I unbuckle my seatbelt, and we head toward the exit. In our luggage we have video cameras, road maps, and ISIS propaganda documents. We're all set—technologically, at least.

To the right of the door, the steward smiles. "I wish you a pleasant stay and hope to see you on board again soon." The gap between the usual polite good-bye and the reality of our own "pleasant stay" is so vast I'm unable to reply, while the Turkish Airlines crew is preparing for its return trip, business as usual. For me and everyone with me, it's clear there will be a "before and after" this journey. I force a tight smile. "See you soon."

THE LION CUBS OF THE CALIPHATE

August 2, 2015—Essian camp

Since our arrival, we have been staying in a hotel in Dohuk, a city in the far north of Iraq, in Kurdistan, near the Syrian and Turkish borders. It is also close to areas under ISIS control. The hotel's façade is dark red, with a sign in silver letters. Inside is a big empty hall, decorated in a Middle Eastern style, and a large, dark restaurant.

When I wake on the first morning, I feel the need to reread, even before breakfast, the notes I took during the long months of preparation for this trip, like a student preparing for an exam. For me, this is a pretty effective way of dealing with apprehension. Before approaching them, I needed to understand who these Yazidis that ISIS is exterminating are.

The geographic area that we're preparing to cross is complex, carved into various entities that either band together or oppose one another—Sunnis, Shiites, Kurds, ISIS, Yazidis—and is riddled with ongoing tensions. Borders have moved. What was formerly Syria has been divided up. The Iraqi army is trying to regain the towns and villages that have come under the control of the terrorist organization. The Yazidis attempted to flee when the Islamic State fighters arrived; those who didn't make it were either killed or reduced to slavery. The territory conquered by ISIS has by force become an entity with Shiites, without Christians, and without Yazidis—other than slaves.

We have done a lot of research on the Yazidis and the chronology of the genocide perpetrated by ISIS in order to have the main points in mind, particularly the dates. The Yazidis are a minority religion within a population that is itself a persecuted minority, the Kurds. In addition to God, the angel Melek Taus plays a central role in their beliefs. Their main place of worship is the temple of Lalish in the province of Nineveh, in northern Iraq. Their religion is passed down orally from parents to children. Geographically, they are mostly present in Iraq and Syria, but there are also some groups in Jordan, Afghanistan, Saudi Arabia, and Afghanistan. A certain number have emigrated to Europe, mostly Germany and Sweden.

In spite of the Yazidis' wish to stay out of the political and religious conflicts that have been ripping Iraq apart since 2003, their relations with Sunni communities have been growing more and more tense. On August 14, 2007, four suicide attacks in the province of Nineveh killed four hundred Yazidis. On August 4, 2014, the city of Sinjar, a major Yazidi center in the northeastern part of Iraq, was conquered by ISIS jihadists, who consider the Yazidis to be infidels, *kuffar.*[1] Tens of thousands of them have sought refuge in Iraqi Kurdistan, but many others have been massacred and thousands kidnapped—five thousand, according to certain sources.

In one year, more than two thousand Yazidis have escaped from the clutches of ISIS.[2] Although some are living in safety in Germany, where they're trying to put their lives back together, the majority of these survivors are getting by in refugee camps in Iraqi Kurdistan. These are whom we're going to see, with the intention of gathering as many eye-witness accounts as possible to give voice to a people being persecuted and massacred for religious reasons in the twenty-first century, and to prove that this is a genocide taking place in the present day.

The car's air conditioner is humming but seems to be struggling. Outside, it's over 104 degrees. Rattled by bumps and potholes, I sink into my seat. I know that in a few days I'll have grown used to little discomforts like these. In the meantime, I suffer in silence and continue to bounce around. We are almost there. In the distance, we see the Essian camp, a stretch of white tents planted on the hillsides.

A distinctive feature of this camp is that it is very long, traversed by a twisty road that is often clogged with traffic. People just passing through come away with their ears ringing from the ambient noise. Taking advantage of the

---

1 The Arab term *kafir* (plural *kuffar*) means someone who doesn't believe in Islam. It is a pejorative term.
2 From the beginning of the genocide in August 2014 to August 2015.

chaos and the needs of the refugees, who number over fifteen thousand in three thousand tents, merchants who are themselves refugees are stationed at every curve of the road, setting up makeshift vegetable stands—tomatoes, onions, cabbages, and peppers—sheltered from the sun by improvised awnings. These little businesses seem to be thriving, as we come upon women carrying heavy sacks filled with food.

One tent that is a bit different catches my eye. It is rectangular, bigger than the others, and some people are waiting at the entrance. I lean close to the window for a better view. I see a dilapidated chair with a mirror, hanging from a thread, facing it. I smile. It is a hair salon. A young man has just been given a stylish cut. Proudly, he checks out the result: right profile, left profile. He runs his hands through the new haircut and nods, visibly satisfied. The scene is both incongruous and comforting. Life endures! It imposes itself within the camp, slowly but surely. Like a plant piercing through concrete, it reclaims its rights.

Zaher brings me back to reality by stating the reason for our visit: "We're going to interview children who have escaped from ISIS camps," he explains. My heart sinks. The bustling activity of the camp hides an ocean of violence and pain. Dark memories hang over it like crows. Our mission is to gather them and communicate them to the world, and I have the feeling it won't be easy. Truth be told, we're charging headlong into the unknown. Indeed, how will we go about interviewing these impoverished young victims who have just escaped from their executioners? And then when that's done, how are we going to make their voices heard, break through indifference so that one day, perhaps, their torturers will face justice? I'm afraid we won't be up to the challenge. But failure isn't an option. Otherwise, the battle will be lost before it's joined.

Learning how to listen takes time. You have to inspire trust, sit still, feel compassion without being overwhelmed by pity, put yourself in the position of a listener while asking the witnesses the questions that will help them remember without directing them, and force yourself not to judge. You have to accompany the witnesses along the roads of their painful past, reconstruct the walls of the prisons in which they were locked up and mistreated, paint the portrait of the people who tried to destroy them.

In the former Soviet Union, on all the roads I traveled, I learned to sit on little low stools in isolated farmsteads to listen to witnesses recount the massacres that had stained the landscapes of their childhood with blood. Staying calm, at least in appearance, without ever batting an eyelid. A certain number of habits acquired during the twenty years I accompanied cancer victims on their final journey—positioning myself at the height of the people I was speaking with, following their rhythms, avoiding looking into the eyes of fragile people—were highly useful for collecting the searing memories of those Russians, Belarusians, and Ukrainians who had witnessed the murders of their Jewish neighbors. Sometimes they were simply bystanders, sometimes participants as well, whether willing or forced.

In Iraq, I've arrived just a year after the beginning of the massacre. This is new for me—genocide in the present. It's not just that these horrors have just been perpetrated or are ongoing but also that the victims are in large part very young. In Eastern Europe, the witnesses were often more than seventy-five years old, yet the scars of their blood-soaked past remained painful. These are two very different situations, I realize, and that is why I'm worried. Nothing has prepared me to listen to the words of a Yazidi who has just escaped from the clutches of ISIS, least of all a child.

Their names are Jotiar, Delgash, and Diar.[3] They are, respectively, nine, eleven, and fifteen years old. They come from ISIS training camps. They wear simple, attractive clothing, brightly colored, no doubt to cancel out the black their jailers made them wear. At first glance, they look no different from other children. Until they begin to speak. Then their bodies start to twitch violently. Their eyes wander here and there, as if on the lookout for a possible enemy. Maintaining eye contact becomes impossible.

Tent A8 [4]

The hot wind of summer in Iraq sweeps into the tent with a soft rustling sound. A woman enters silently, barefoot, and sets a small bottle of cold water in front of each of us. I look sidewise at Jotiar, without staring. I've briefed the others to do the same. It's essential that the witness never feels hemmed

---

3   For security reasons, all the names have been changed.
4   For security reasons, the numbers of the tents and trailers have been changed.

in, even by our stares. The family is sitting nearby, near the entrance, ears perked. Jotiar appears fairly calm, but the closer we get to the moment he has to speak, as we prepare our photographic equipment, the more jerky his movements and breathing become. The uncontrollable twitching of the muscles in his face reveal his unease. He tries to smile.

Jotiar had been a prisoner of ISIS for more than a year. He's only nine years old—as if to convince himself, he keeps repeating this over and over. Clumsily, not really knowing where to begin or how to act, I start the interview with a gaffe: I ask him which village he lived in when he was little.

No sooner have I uttered the question than I regret having asked it. He is still "little." In France, he would be in grade school, learning the basics of grammar and spelling, arithmetic, history, and geography. Here he has learned how to kill and how to die. Having been trained in an ISIS camp takes away one's childhood but doesn't cause one to grow up. He's still a child.

The rest of the conversation piles one gaffe on top of another. We're all embarrassed to be adults, five of us facing a young boy recounting the way his carefree childhood has been sucked away by the dark folly of grown-ups.

Jotiar doesn't seem to hold my tactlessness against me and answers without holding back. He grew up in Hardan, a village in the northern part of Iraq. Without being asked, he adds, "One of my cousins betrayed me. He sold me to ISIS." That was in August 2014. He was on his way to visit a Sunni friend when the ISIS men approached his village. "It was our friend who phoned ISIS to come capture us," he spat out in rage. His serious tone and the anger I heard in his voice clash with his childish face. "He betrayed us," he repeats. I sigh.

At the age of nine, Jotiar ought to be suffering the little dramas of childhood—unfair fights between friends, stolen marbles, a secret love revealed. He shouldn't be experiencing the deadly weightiness of the word "betrayal"—by a friend, a neighbor—the true offense and wound that cannot be healed.

Jotiar was then caught and driven away in a car. He was only eight. I have trouble following the names of the villages and the towns he mentions. He was transported in vans and buses with curtains drawn, thrown from one vehicle to another like some kind of ordinary parcel.

Overcome with emotion, he speaks confusedly. He describes a difficult moment, when he is separated from the girls and women of his family. The interpreter interrupts him to clarify this frantic tale: "In your bus, how old was the youngest child? And the oldest?" The answer is devastating: "Almost everyone was eleven years old. I was eight."

Suddenly, the little boy is carried away by his memories. He talks without pausing, and I have the impression he can no longer stop himself. He pours out a stream of choppy phrases to describe the repeated training sessions and the systematic violence to which he was subjected. Then Jotiar calms down as abruptly as he flared up. He takes a breath. He puts words to the scenes of his life that emerge from his memory. In a confused jumble, he describes the months of his captivity.

I finally understand the reason for the haze surrounding Jotiar's story: white pills that the jailers gave the youngest children every night, inspecting their mouths to make sure they were swallowing them properly. The two men who gave out the drugs were the same ones doing the training and the beating. Their names would come up again in the stories told by other children. They were apparently the heads of the recruitment system of the camp in which Jotiar was locked up.

I hazard a question: "Did you take the pills willingly?" Without hesitating he answers, "The pills made me strong." In the language of his young age, he's acknowledging that this daily dose of drugs gave him pleasure and the relief of forgetting.

I recall arrests in Turkey of traffickers of a drug intended for ISIS. I recall that it was Captagon, an amphetamine that improves brain function and confers a feeling of omnipotence but is highly addictive. I don't know whether what Jotiar was taking was Captagon, but I imagine that after his return from the camp the little boy must have suffered withdrawal symptoms. Craving a drug they've been forced to take and then suffering cruelly when it's taken away—what conflicting feelings!

For the family of the little boy, his return isn't easy to manage. Being reunited with them is surely a huge relief, but the trauma remains, and the most innocuous events—someone entering abruptly, the arrival of a car—constantly awaken memories in him. He thinks he sees the ISIS men who supervised the camp. It will take time for the son who came back safe and sound to find true deliverance. At night, he still sleeps in the fields, just in case the ISIS men return.

This first conversation plunges me into a state of total confusion. I had prepared myself for this first meeting with a child victim. I'd been expecting tears, hatred, fear, primal anger, the kinds of extreme feelings one surely has at that age. But that hasn't been the case at all. Jotiar's account is surprisingly nuanced. He'll never forgive the childhood friend who betrayed him and sold him to ISIS; he hasn't forgotten the wrenching separation from his family, nor the pain of the beatings or the hardships of the training. Nevertheless, in the wave of emotions that washes over him as he speaks, it's hard to find a trace of anger or a desire for vengeance. Valy, too, is perplexed. As soon as we leave the tent, he tells the rest of the team, "I don't understand how he can speak in such detail about what he has lived through without seeming to feel some deep emotion!" We're all asking ourselves the same question. We talk it over for a long time and then decide to continue. We have to learn, step by step, without running, to take control of these interviews. Take the time to discuss and share our impressions, adapt our method. This isn't our last surprise, nor our last self-questioning.

Tent A26

I know from experience that witnesses, whether children or adults, can make up stories, sometimes involuntarily. That's why I'm in the habit of posing the same questions to several witnesses who have lived through the same situation, in this case other children who stayed in the same camp as Jotiar.

Diar is older. He was fourteen when he was kidnapped by men from ISIS. He's wearing the tee-shirt of a Barcelona soccer player. As with Jotiar, when we get to the drugs they were given, I ask, "Do you have the impression that the medicines tired you out or that they made you strong?" He doesn't answer right away; he takes time to think about it. "Actually, we didn't feel anything. We felt like we were ISIS. Sometimes I imagine I'm still with them. I often have headaches. I pass out."

The drug seems to have had a much stronger effect on Diar than on Jotiar, and he still feels the aftereffects today. The white pills made him forget his Yazidi identity. He felt like he was fully a member of ISIS, and he was proud of it. He still seems to feel that way. The forcible drugging in the children's camps makes me wonder. Indeed, all the children we met were drugged regularly, for months, which never ceases to surprise me. The administration of intoxicants is a systematic practice by ISIS on the young prisoners the organization is trying to indoctrinate. This method is obviously at odds with the ideology being promoted, which forbids the consumption of alcohol; people can be tried and convicted for smoking or listening to Western music. I don't see how, without contravening the religious precepts it so loudly proclaims, ISIS can countenance drug consumption, voluntary or not—even if it isn't for recreational use, as they say, but in the service of an ultimate goal. Using it to convert young recruits also implies that propaganda isn't enough to incite the conversion of its targets.

Along with the drugs, the Koran and the precepts of the caliphate were drummed into the children. Did ISIS suspect that its ideology alone wouldn't be enough to persuade Yazidi youngsters to become apprentice terrorists? Did the organization doubt the effectiveness of its Islamist ideology?

It seems to me that the soldiers of the caliphate, clear-sighted as they are about the inadequacy of their religious discourse to deal with their "slaves," are putting medicine and its almost magical powers in service to their ideas, which in themselves aren't potent enough to indoctrinate the prisoners and brainwash them. Drugs have come to the rescue of the religion that's being forced on them. "Religion is the opium of the people," declared Marx in 1843. To this maxim, ISIS has added drugs.

To me, the decision to drug children sheds light on the full personal responsibility of these radical Islamists. They are criminals who know full well what they're doing. Fanatical though they may be, blinded by their extreme faith, they're not so incapable of realistic reflection as to forget that in order for their convictions to take root, they must complement the conversion process with a thoroughly modern chemical catalyst for the transplant to hold. The Islamic State is at once archaic and scientific, fanatical and infinitely practical.

Besides this double mental coercion, the extremist interpretation of the Koran and the daily ingestion of drugs, there are the beatings. Diar and one of his young brothers, Delgash, attempted to escape. They failed. The punishment was harsh: 250 lashes divided between the two children. To spare his little brother, Diar begged to be able to bear them all. "My brother was too young, he would have died." The jailer agreed. "They hung me from a metal bar, and then they whipped me 250 times." Diar and his little brother never again tried to escape.

The ISIS training camps are machines for breaking the bodies and burgeoning minds of children until they forget where they came from, until they feel close to their executioners and their ideas and are ready to fight for them, in life and death. They are then called "the lion cubs of the caliphate."

Delgash, the little brother, is now eleven years old. He appears alert; he, too, wears a soccer tee-shirt. He's proud of his big brother and eager to give his version of the events: "My brother got beaten in front of all the other kids in the camp. . . . I cried while I watched him." This punishment was thus an example designed to discourage other escape attempts. Delgash continues with the story: "That wasn't the first time. Another time they gave 250 lashes to a ten-year-old, and the next day he was found dead."

Excerpt from the Interview with Jotiar

Did you have weapons?
Yes, we had weapons.

What kind of weapons?
Kalashnikovs.

Were they heavy?
No, they were light; they gave us light weapons.

Were they real or fake weapons?
They were real weapons.

Did you learn to shoot?
Yes.

What did you shoot at?
We shot at silhouettes.

Were they cardboard men? Wooden?
Wooden.

Were you supposed to shoot at the head or at the body?
They told us to shoot anywhere.

Were you able to aim or not?
Yes, I was able to.

**And what did they tell you? That the wooden man
was a Peshmerga?**
Yes, they told us they were Peshmergas.[5]

**And when you aimed well were you supposed to
shout something?**
Yes, they told us to shout, "Allahu Akbar."

Did you ever shoot a real person they brought out?
No.

Always wooden men?
Yes.

Did they also teach you how to attack a house?
Yes.

How did you attack a house?
We attacked from both sides.

How did you get the door open?
If the door didn't open, we shot at the lock.

Was there anyone in the house?
No, no one was there.

---

5 The term *Peshmerga* is used by the Kurds to designate their fighters,
who were the central elements of the fight against ISIS in Iraq.
The regional government of Kurdistan also uses it as a name for
the armed forces of Iraqi Kurdistan. In Kurdish the word *Peshmerga*
means "he who faces death."

What did you do when you entered the house?
We went in quietly; we searched all the rooms.

Did they teach you how to transport bombs in the streets?
Yes.

How big were those bombs? Can you show it to us with your hands?
They were very big.

Were they heavy?
Yes, they were very heavy.

And where did you put them?
We dug in roads and we put them in the holes.

Did you learn to dig holes in the road, or did someone else do it?
It was ISIS that did it.

And how did you plant them?
Only one at a time, and we put some in every street. About five bombs in each street.

What was the name of the village where you put the bombs?
Hay Al-Kedra.

And the village was empty?
Yes, no one was there.

Were the children the only ones who planted the bombs?
We planted the bombs, and they hid them.

Did you get the bombs from a crate?
The bombs were in plastic bags packed in the crate.

Did you have to cut the plastic?
We put them down with the plastic.

Do you think those bombs exploded? Did they show you any videos?
They told us, "These bombs are going to blow up the Peshmergas' cars."

For how many days did you plant bombs?
We worked for two days on a street.

And were all those streets in the same village?
Yes.

While you were transporting the bombs, did the adults back off?
Yes.

Were there any accidents? Did some boys die because of the bombs?
Yes.

Did you see a boy get blown up by a bomb?
Yes.

Was it a boy you knew?
No.

Was he your age?
Yes, he was my age.

Why did he get blown up? Did he make a mistake with the bomb?
The bomb fell from his hands, and it exploded before he put it into the hole. He didn't know that the bomb was going to explode.

If someone dropped it into the hole, was there a chance that the bomb might explode?
Yes.

Did you have to put it down very gently?
Yes, we were very careful when we put them down.

What did they do with the body of the boy who died?
They buried it at the side of the road.

Were there any other times when children died?
Several times. I remember two times.

Where were the men when the children were placing the bombs? Did they hide behind the trucks?
They went far away from us.

Did they talk to you with loudspeakers when they gave you orders?
Yes, they spoke to us with loudspeakers.

Where did they keep the crate of bombs? In the car or near the holes?
In the car.

So the children got the bombs out of the cars, and then they put them in the holes?
Yes.

That day, there were how many children?
About thirty.

All boys?
Yes.

Did there need to be two children to carry a bomb, or could one child do it himself?
Two.

And it took two children to put it in the hole too?
No, just one.

So, two children carried the bomb from the car to the hole, and then one child alone put it down.
Yes.

And you weren't afraid because of the pills, right?
No. I was always afraid.

Do you remember how many days you spent putting the bombs into the holes?
Fifty days.

After you had set the bombs correctly, did they give you anything?
They said, "Your work here is finished. We are going to take you back to your mothers."

In the evenings, when you came back, did they congratulate you for having done a good job?
Yes, they gave us milk and bread.

And when a child died by getting blown up, did you stop working or did you have to keep going?
We kept working.

Do you think it was the pills that kept you strong?
Yes.

Did the pills make you forget what you had done the day before?
No, I didn't forget.

And so, after fifty days they brought you back to your mothers?

Yes.

THE CHILDREN BACK
FROM THE CAMPS

August 3, 2015—Kadia camp

The hotel's aquarium gives off a dull light. Inside it, over-sized fish are trying to move around a bit. The guards are waiting, leaning back in the worn leather armchairs of the immense reception area. It's breakfast time.

As I'm hurrying to go join the team, eyes and mind still sleepy, I notice that the security men responsible for our safety look a bit worried. Usually Subhi, the head of the unit, a Kurd from Erbil, gets up to greet me. Today, he looks somber, distracted, lost in thought. Zaher, who is always perky, is already at the table, with an odd feast in front of him. His plate is filled with almonds covered with a mixture of honey and sesame paste.

I sit down and question him: "Zaher, is there a problem?"

"No," he responds without looking up.

For Zaher, who fled his country to escape an imminent massacre, there's never any real problem anymore. Changing neither his expression nor his intonation, he explains, "This is the anniversary of the beginning of the genocide. It seems like things are going to be heating up in the camps. The guards told me."

I say nothing. I'm served a cup of local espresso. I think about what Zaher has said, weighing the pros and cons. So many times, along roads in Ukraine, people have told me it wasn't the right day, the right time, the right place to find witnesses to the genocide of the Jews. I can still hear the voices of those *kolkhoz* farm women in blue smocks, standing in a muddy road: "You're wasting your time; there's no one old enough left here; they are all dead." In other places, while we looked for somewhere to stay, a villager would tell me that access to the town was forbidden under the Soviets because military vessels were being built there. "There are no hotels here. You ought to leave." I always persevered in those cases, and I was right to do so. A few dozen meters away from the farm women in smocks, in the same street, I would find an old lady, a ninety-year-old grandmother eager to talk to us. And farther on, a ten-story gray concrete hotel, typical Soviet style, would dominate the central square.

Now once again, on a day that has barely begun, when nobody knows what's going to happen, I'm standing before Zaher, who is perhaps thinking this might not be the right day, that on this sad anniversary, it might be too dangerous to go to the camp, that we might just be better off staying in the hotel and waiting until tomorrow. I lower my head, as if to push ahead, and tell myself, "We're going, you'll see."

This stubbornness has been a part of my makeup for a long time. I was a wild child, and my mother used to complain about my contrariness to the customers of our little store in Chalon-sur-Saône: "When you want him to close the door, you have to tell him to open it, and then he'll close it!" Rebellious as a child, I was already inhabited by a refusal of limits, of fences, of being closed in, that has never left me. Later, at the age of thirteen, sitting alone on a wooden chair at the end of the dining-room table, I would leaf through catalogues from travel agencies that I'd "borrowed." One night, my father caught me daydreaming, fascinated by images of infinite colorful deserts. "You know very well you'll never leave!" he exclaimed. I waited until I was of age. Starting when I was eighteen, I worked in the recycling furnaces of the Kodak factory. With the money I earned there, to the consternation of my family, I took a vacation to the oases of Algeria with a friend.

I think I'm still that obstinate child, but thanks to my teachers, both within and outside the Church, I've learned to channel my stubbornness and put it in service of a goal. Today, I use it to overcome barriers that spring up and open the doors that systematically close when you're trying to dig up a truth that has been willfully buried.

My coffee is bitter and cold, and I gulp it down as best I can. Then I make a decision: "Zaher, we are leaving at 8:30." I announce this also to Valy and Victoria, who arrive a little bit later, still wrapped in the morning fog that I've just shaken off: "We are going to Kadia!" Maybe it's crazy, a foolish risk. I don't know what awaits us.

The white cars set off for the camp. The guards are silent, concentrating, the walkie-talkies buzzing with brief messages. They haven't challenged my decision and are pre-paring themselves mentally to keep us safe, whatever the cir-cumstances. As we approach Kadia, I suddenly notice long plastic-coated signs clattering in the wind, barely attached to the barbed wire by little pieces of string. A portrait of a Yazidi child, face covered in tears, and GENOCIDE! written in red letters that look like blood, a silent plaint addressed to the world, spread over ragged signs. My blood freezes.

Yazidi children observe us, their faces somber and sad, with a handful of string under their arms, probably for hang-ing up more silent appeals for help. At the end of a long, dusty, unpaved road, the victims of genocide cry out to an indifferent wind. They watch us enter the camp, Western witnesses from outside. In their eyes is an infinite question: since we're there, since we're aware, are we going to help them? In that instant, I feel the weight of our responsibility to make the world hear their cry. There, not very far away, out in the Iraqi and Syrian countryside, ISIS is exterminat-ing a people.

"Shvan is waiting for us," says Souhaib, the red-haired young man accompanying us, who is seated at the back of the vehicle.

"Who's that?" I ask without turning around, for fear of being bounced around too much over the sharp turns on the dusty road.

"A young man who has just escaped from the training camps. He was filmed in an ISIS propaganda video. Look!"

Souhaib hands me his little black telephone. On the screen is a young ISIS member with long hair and a thick beard, dressed all in black. Alongside him are children kneeling, likewise in black, each one wearing a headband. Souhaib points to a face just to the side of the "master," or should I say "owner," which is probably what he considers himself to be? I force myself to concentrate, to look closely at this face in spite of the car's bouncing. I have a hard time making out the details. The child's eyes are lowered, squinting under the black headband, and he looks stifled. The car finally stops, in the full sun, and we go meet the 108-degree heat of August.

Valy and Zaher walk ahead, stepping quickly. I'm having trouble following them. I don't feel well because of the searing heat, perhaps also because of my age, and maybe also because I'm apprehensive about what is to come. Concentrating on the upcoming account of a Yazidi survivor, my body refuses to move quickly. Yesterday's conversations have shaken me. I've found children who are victims of the madness of ISIS, but I've also glimpsed the fearsome efficiency of their methods of recruitment. These children are victims first of all, but they are also apprentice terrorists whose free will has been destroyed. I want to pierce the secrets of ISIS, while at the same time I am reluctant to let go of my comfortable ignorance. This is what always happens. I start my research with a certain number of theories in my head, which soon give way to a more complicated reality.

When I enter the trailer, barefoot out of respect for local customs and for the sake of cleanliness, the boy, Shvan, is already seated. Not moving, he stares fixedly at me. His black hair forms a sort of helmet, giving him something of a military look. Right away he strikes me as different from the other children I've met since our arrival.

We have barely set up our equipment when he gets down to the facts, without flinching. "I am fourteen years old, and I come from Kojo. I ran away from ISIS eight days ago." He describes his life during the six months he spent on the other side of the border, a camp that, as I can see from his eyes, he has not yet left totally behind.

For this teenager, the camp is, first of all, the place where he was forced to convert to Islamist ideology. One name keeps coming back: Abu O., the man who taught him Arabic and forced him to learn to read the Koran. "He was slim, had a big beard and long hair." I seem to detect a hint of admiration when he speaks of his "master," similar to the way a Western child talks about his idol. This is all the more troubling in that Shvan is recalling the beatings he got when he was unable to memorize the precepts being inculcated. "Anyone who didn't know how to read, they hit him with wooden sticks."

As he recalls the stages of his captivity, the method of indoctrination used in the ISIS training camp becomes clearer: long days without stopping, ideas—or rather slogans—hammered in endlessly, with screams and beatings to drive them home.

On arrival in the camp, the children's heads were shaved by their jailers, a practice that drew my attention. Is tonsure a rite of passage, the first step in entering the camp? The hair that has been cut off and then discarded is the symbol of the former life, whereas the new haircut makes them all look alike. Henceforth, they were no longer individuals but bearers of a grand "revolutionary" movement. From then on, they belonged to ISIS. "Level one, the lowest setting of the shears," Shvan recalls. Then the children put on the green and gray uniform, along with the headband marked with the "slogan" of their new homeland: LA ILAHA ILLA ALLAH. (There is no god but God.)

The distribution of equipment to the ISIS recruits, whether they are volunteers or forced, is well organized and precise. Each is given an identical package. Everything is carefully planned and recorded.

I can't help noticing how much they look like the thousands of children I encountered in Burkina Faso during the revolution in 1983. At that time, I was a math teacher in Dédougou. One evening the rickety taxi I was taking to visit a French development aide in an isolated neighborhood stopped suddenly and refused to go any further, stranding me far from my destination. On the road, twelve-year-olds, dressed in military uniforms and heavily armed, were searching all the cars. These children, most of whom had never gone to school, were the "guardians" of the revolution, and they took their role very seriously. I was trudging through the killer heat with my heavy suitcase when, weapons in hand, they signaled me to stop. After shouting the national slogan, "Country or death, we shall prevail!" they led me to an improvised sentry booth and grabbed my passport. My only fear was that it would disappear. They examined it, brows furrowed in concentration, but I noticed that they were holding it upside down, as they clearly didn't know how to read.

This anecdote, amusing in retrospect, didn't strike me as funny at the time. A child who has been granted authority and a Kalashnikov is a fearsome thing. When one allows and orders a child to kill in the name of a cause that he has been indoctrinated to feel is just, he can do monstrous things. And the little guardians of the revolution did commit their share of atrocities. Often, in conflicts in this part of the world, impressionable children are the first to be transformed into legal assassins for the new regime.

Listening to a young boy recount the way he has been trained to kill and to die presents a tough challenge. Indeed, we must simultaneously take into consideration the child he still is and the potential killer he has become, without reducing him to just one of those facets. The first camp Shvan was taken to was in Tal Afar, but it was only when he was transferred to Raqqa that his training began in earnest, first with the physical conditioning—enduring the pain of beatings, running, jumping, crawling—and then the handling of weapons and bombs.

"The ISIS men told us, 'You're going to learn to use weapons in order to fight.'"

"And what weapon did you have?"

"A Kalashnikov. I kept it even at night, when patrolling the camp with the ISIS fighters. Even at those times I had my Kalashnikov. We took it apart; we put it back together again."

I'm astounded. He speaks with the voice of a fourteen-year-old, but his exact words are those of an experienced soldier calmly describing his technical training. One sentence caught my attention: he had to guard the camp at night. Does that mean that this young boy had somehow become a trusted aide in the eyes of his superiors? Too many questions run through my mind, and I have to concentrate to go on listening to Shvan.

I would later learn that the training camp guards designated certain children in each room as "emirs" responsible for supervising the others, denouncing the "errors" they committed, and then determining their punishments. These emirs are children who have the right and the responsibility to strike the others. In the dictatorship concocted by ISIS, even the victims are ensnared in hierarchical echelons of violence.

Listing to him, I think about the terrorists in Paris and elsewhere, who have probably learned and rehearsed the same acts—how to endure pain, plant bombs, assemble and take apart an assault rifle, load it, aim it, and fire it—in order to kill.

Shvan goes on with his account, mechanically reciting the list of "toughening sessions" preceding weapons training. "The hardest for me was when they walked on my belly. Also, we couldn't scream. If we did, they would hit us." I shudder: the child sitting across from me has been maltreated in order to inure him to the pain inflicted by his guards. "We shot at targets. When we hit them, they said, 'That's good!' The targets were shaped like people; they were cut-outs. It wasn't hard."

Over and over, insistently and firmly, he repeats, with a touch of pride, "It wasn't hard." I understand that his body and his heart, hardened by beatings, haven't entirely left the camp.

Liberated from ISIS, safely inside the camp's white refugee trailer and among members of his family, he still speaks like an apprentice terrorist: "It wasn't difficult." Shvan was transformed into a very good shot, able to hit the target in the heart. His sole objective, once indoctrinated, was to do well so his bosses would congratulate him, for even though ISIS guards excel in the art of punishment, they also know how to dole out rewards. The basic principles of training are to punish the child when he fails to do what he's supposed to do and reward him when he does well, until he has internalized the system of "values" and is no longer even able to think.

There is one question I can't stop thinking about: why does this terrorist organization, ISIS, incorporate within itself large numbers of Yazidi children? To avoid sacrificing its own children, even though it holds up martyrdom as the supreme destiny? To punish the ancient people of Sinjar, who have been resisting it, by alienating the identity of their sons? But why then would it offer the people it considers to be *kuffar*, even those who have converted, a pathway to paradise? It seems to me that religion alone doesn't explain all these paradoxes.

The soldiers of ISIS aren't just religious fanatics who make sense of the world by organizing their surroundings into legalistic religious categories. They are also warriors. They have conquered a vast territory in Iraq and Syria, have imposed their laws on it, and are trying, through battles and massacres, to extend it even further. They're at war with the West, their own Rome, the embodiment of everything they abhor. There are no wars, including religious ones, that don't have strategies.

I recall the faces of Jotiar, Delgash, and Diar. Some of them, like Shvan, have Western features. Some are blond, with faces that would blend in easily among us in France, where they could obtain refugee status that would open doors to them. Could ISIS be looking beyond Iraq and Syria, projecting long-term into the future and training these young terrorists in view of "exporting" them?

That very evening I would call CBS investigative reporter Lara Logan in Washington, who was to confirm my intuition: "They are cultivating them! For the future!"

This is ISIS as a business enterprise on the rise, mass-producing little terrorists to flood the international market. It is a terrifying theory, as yet unverifiable.

For now, I must pull myself together and finish the interview, in spite of the stifling heat that's making me drowsy. I'm having trouble listening and analyzing at the same time so I can ask pertinent questions. "They taught us how to hold grenades and throw them so they would explode. We had some kind of vests with pockets. There was a pin. If you pulled it, the grenade would blow up." Unconsciously, while he is talking, his arms, his hands, his whole body mime precisely the gestures of a grenade thrower. An automaton.

"How many grenades did you have on you?"

"Two. They were like this," says Shvan, tracing out the shape with his hands. "The ISIS men would tell us, 'You're going to throw them at the enemies.' And we had to pull out the pins."

"Were they real grenades?"

"Real ones," he says without batting an eyelid. "They told us, 'When you fight, you will be throwing them at infidels, apostates.'"

Religion permeates the training. The enemy to be eliminated is an "apostate." Does this Islamist terminology regarding the "others" denote a constellation of religious ideals to be realized in the future, or is it simply a pretext to justify murders and persuade children to commit them?

Unfortunately, I think ISIS members believe so strongly in the worldview they've created that large numbers of them are willing to die in order to hasten its advent.

My thoughts are far from Shvan. He lists the names of the camps to which he was transferred successively during his training to escape bombardments. "Every time we heard a plane we switched camps." Two names come up often, Sular and Raqqa. He's vague about their precise locations within the towns, as if still bound by the obligation to maintain ISIS secrets. These camps are often former schools or administrative buildings, above ground or below, but they are apparently temporary bases that can be evacuated at the least hint of danger overhead. The real jails are the guards and the prisoners, not the walls.

Shvan spells out the draconian rules governing the lives of the children in these temporary camps. Punishments were doled out at the least misconduct: "If someone was smoking, they would beat him with a wooden stick in front of all the others. They threw him on the ground, and they beat him. They tied up his hands and hit the soles of his feet."

I interrupt him. There's something in his story that I don't understand. "And were his feet tied up, too?"

"No. They would make us hold his feet."

His answer is a shock. My suspicions are confirmed: Shvan has personally participated in the torture of other Yazidi children. This is profoundly troubling. Was he a true believer in ISIS or a tool exploited by them? I'm getting a more complete picture of who he is: a teenager, who has participated, willingly or not, in the camp's way of life, in oppressing his own people. He was probably an emir of the camp, responsible for keeping the others in line. So much for the naïve fantasies of dreamers who imagine that in human beings there is a line between innocence on one side and guilt on the other. In times of totalitarian war and violent oppression, the line blurs, and the rules of common decency give way.

I think of my grandfather Claudius, deported to Camp 325 in Rawa Ruska in the Ukraine. The prisoners were forced to dig the mass graves of Jews. What did my grandfather do? Did he dig? I carry with me the memory of an ancestor who was deported, and who, in order to survive, had to carry out the orders of his torturers. Valy, seated at my left, also has inherited a painful memory: the silence of family members who survived the camp at Kavaliovka while so many others were lying in huge mass graves.

Recounting what he has gone through and what he has put others through, Shvan is making us face ourselves and the memories of deported families. Torture degrades the body and the soul, and trying to separate out black from white is a fallacy.

I have to insist that Shvan give us the names of the people who beat up the children. He is reticent, as though revealing this were still dangerous. Or is it rather that a bond has been formed between the masters and the disciple, and that he wants to protect them? Yes, perhaps he doesn't want to betray them. He ends up giving us two names, Abu Q. and Abu M.—noms de guerre—and then he adds, "They were also the ones who taught us the Koran."

Religion classes given by those who punish, forced complicity, forbidden things, weapons, intensive training. This is how ISIS warps the bodies and consciences of Yazidi children. The goal is not only to break them but to cause a triple transformation: religious, military, and terrorist.

I have to catch my breath.

I need a break.

After Jotiar, Diar, Delgash, and Shvan, we meet many other young survivors of ISIS camps. We realize that the return of the children to their families doesn't just bring relief, a happy ending. It's also a lucrative business. The parents are usually contacted by a smuggler. A ransom is demanded, often in the neighborhood of $1,500, to buy back their child. To raise that much money, the parents scrounge through the refugee camps, borrow here and there, go into debt.

Once the child returns, the families feel helpless. He's no longer the boy who was stolen from them. One mother tells us that her son is still acting like a member of ISIS. "Every morning when he wakes up, he wants to dress like them. He insults the Yazidis, calls us *kuffar*." A grandmother tells us that her nine-year-old grandson has forgotten Kurdish and speaks nothing but Arabic.

In the refugee camps, there is psychological assistance, but not enough. When a mother reports that her children have become very aggressive, she is simply told that "it will take time" for the effects of indoctrination and drugs to wear off. Most of the parents prefer to keep quiet and wait, hoping that time will heal, that someday their son will behave normally again.

The descriptions of the training camps vary greatly from one witness to another. We end up realizing that there isn't just one standard ISIS camp. Some informants mention schools, some speak of underground camps. We therefore decide to ask each child to draw the camp he was kept in on a large sheet of white paper. This method works well, for some of the youngsters have trouble talking and the pencil jogs their memory. At the same time, it allows us to see if their memories square with those of the others. Such is the case with Zana, whom we interview several months after Shvan, during our second trip.

He is from Wadi al-Hajar, and he is now fifteen years old. His long stay in ISIS camps has destroyed whatever was left of his innocence and traumatized him. He was trained in several camps in Syria and Iraq. On the white sheet of paper spread out on the ground, he has drawn walls, guard towers on both sides of the entrance, rooms for storing weapons, the locations of the shooters and the cushions on which they could lie down (sometimes five at once), baths, and toilets.

The sketch is detailed and precise. I'm surprised to see electrical installations covering the roof of the camp. "Like in a soccer stadium," says Zana. This isn't an insignificant detail. In Iraq, power outages happen all the time, which the men of ISIS seem to have anticipated, as though technical problems of that sort were never allowed to disturb the smooth operation of the camp. I ask for specifics. "We had light inside, and there were projectors, one in each corner. There was an electric generator and solar panels too. During the day, they took the solar panels outdoors." It seems that, contrary to what the stories about frequent relocations to escape the threat of bombardments had led us to believe, the camps weren't makeshift structures made to be abandoned. These sites were a central element in the strategy of ISIS and were equipped with modern fixtures that allowed them to operate day and night, much like a factory where, to optimize production, the machines operate nonstop. It seems that the education of young terrorists is an absolute priority. The training camps for children are the future of ISIS.

Zana continues drawing frenetically. Naturally, he draws only the things he was able to see—Yazidi children often enter the camps blindfolded—and understand. We make out ropes suspended from the roof of the camp. "That's to train us to shimmy up with an explosive belt, grenades, and a Kalashnikov." He explains that he had to choose a weapon. He decided to become a sniper, whereas one of his friends preferred to learn to shoot a pistol. Certain boys "specialize" in armed attacks on residential areas, while others become concealed shooters, still others bomb planters, and so forth.

The trainers wrote his name on a piece of paper, which was then glued to his weapon. He then had to pass tests: he fired seven bullets but wasn't good enough to be chosen. "The ten best boys were selected," he sighs wistfully.

Because he wasn't a good shot, Zana had to undergo further training in another camp, still with the hope of becoming a sniper. He was never selected and ended up studying in an ISIS school, where he was labeled unsuited for combat. I understand that the camp authorities considered him to be one of the worst shooters, while he was also one of the oldest. A tragedy for a teenager.

Being a bad shot may have saved his life, but his self-image still suffers from the sight of others succeeding where he failed repeatedly. "Loading the rifle and carrying it was hard. It was heavy. I failed at being a shooter. The ones who were good shots got taken away, I don't know where."

The young shooters who were selected left the camp as heroes, without blindfolds, which makes me think ISIS used them as combatants. But where did they go? No one ever saw them again. "Sent abroad," if the terse explanation of the "selector" was to be believed. Into combat zones? Transformed into suicide troops? Destined for attacks in the West in the long term?

Before folding up Zana's sketch to put it in my bag, I glance at it one last time. It isn't a child's drawing.

Excerpt from the Interview with Shvan

Were the grenades they gave you fake or real?
Real.

Did you throw them far?
Yes, far.

Did you do the training outdoors?
Yes.

Did they teach you to throw the grenades at something?
No. They told us, "When you fight, you will throw them at infidels."

Did they teach you to throw the grenades into houses, through the windows, as if you were attacking?
Yes.

How did you attack a house? Did you only throw grenades? Or did some of you carry weapons?
Yes, we had weapons too. They told us, "When you're in combat, as soon as you're out of bullets, you must throw the grenades."

So you had both grenades and weapons.
Yes.

Did you have to learn to run while carrying the weapons and the grenades?
Yes, they made us carry them, even if we couldn't do it.

Did they send you into a real military battle?
No, just training.

How many places did they take you to?
Every time we heard the planes, we went to a different place.

Did you move to a new place before the plane arrived?
Each time the plane bombed near us, we went to a different place.

Were you warned ahead of time about the bombings?
Yes, they communicated with each other with their walkie-talkies.

Were you able to get a cell phone?
No.

Were any boys able to keep a cell phone?
No. If they knew someone had one, they hit him.

Were certain things against the rules? Like smoking, for example?
Smoking was forbidden.

Were there any boys who got punished because they had been smoking or drinking?
Every time a boy caused a problem, they hit him.

What did they hit him with?
A wooden stick.

Did they hit him in front of everybody?
Yes, so everyone could see and they wouldn't make any more trouble.

Did they tie them up before they hit them?
They tied their hands.

Feet, too?
No, they made us hold the feet of the boy being punished.

Where did they hit him?
They would hit the soles of his feet.

While he was being punished, was the boy lying down or hanging?
They hit him on the ground.

Did the boy have to count the number of times he was hit?
No, they didn't count. They hit as much as they wanted to.

When they hit a boy in front of you, did you cry or scream, or were you not allowed to?

No, we couldn't.

Did any boys try to escape?

No.

Did they show you how to plant bombs?

No, I didn't learn how.

And the explosives belts, did they show them to you?

Yes, we had them.

Were they heavy?

Yes, they were heavy.

What did they used to tell you?

They told us, "You will put them on when you have to fight."

Do you remember when they came to photograph and film you?

Yes.

Did they ask you to make certain gestures, or could you do as you liked?

They were the ones who told us how to position ourselves and what gestures to make.

Were the movie cameras like the ones cameramen have, with feet?
Yes, a little higher.

How long did the filming take?
About an hour.

Did they film you often?
They came once. They filmed us while we were training.

Do you remember that day? Did they come in the morning or the afternoon?
The morning.

And did your leader tell you that you should be well dressed because the cameraman was going to come?
Yes, they told us ahead of time, and later they checked to be sure that we were dressed right.

Was there someone behind the camera to show you what gestures to make?
Yes, there was.

Who was that?
Abu O., our trainer.

If a boy did well in training, did they give him a reward? Did he become a leader?
No, they gave him things.

What kind of things?

Money.

How much money did they give him?

Ten thousand Syrian pounds. That makes twenty thousand Iraqi dinars.[6]

What could you buy with that amount? Was there anyone selling things around the camp?

They bought things for us.

Did they ever give you any money?

Yes, once.

And what did you ask for?

I asked for a phone.

Did you get it?

No, they gave me some cookies.

And how did all this end? How were you able to get out?

Somebody bought me. He came with a paper and took me to my mother.

Did the person who came with the paper already know your first name?

My mother had told him my name.

---

6   About US$17, a significant sum for the boy.

Did they let you leave easily? Without asking any questions?
They said, "You can take him."

How long have you been out?
About a week.

Was the man who came to get you a member of ISIS?
Yes.

How did you get out? Where did you go?
We went over the Turkish border.

Do you still have images and memories of the training in your head?
No.

Do you like it better here or there?
Here.

THE MASS GRAVES

August 4, 2015—Kadia camp
Trailer D12

The blinding light and suffocating heat are settling in. Shielding my eyes, I try to make out the scene stretching before me. A huge village of white trailers as far as the eye can see, gleaming, perched on cement pilings, divided by immaculately clean white gravel into little sections. Women and young girls wearing dark clothing are sweeping. On the ground, not a bit of trash, not a single scrap of paper. Some families have constructed makeshift awnings to provide a bit of shade.

Each "house" is decorated with the enormous round blue logo of the Rwanga Foundation, whose mission is to aid refugees form Kurdistan, Iraq, and elsewhere. Outside the camp, on the other side of the gate, is a bunch of stands, tiny shops that carry provisions for the families. Under the blazing sun, men, women, and children all lug enormous plastic sacks, filled to the brim, to their rudimentary dwellings.

The camp at Kadia is immense, a small city carved out of towering mountains at the end of a long, winding, unpaved road. White dust, kicked up by the cars, twists around and envelops each of the vehicles in our convoy, making them almost invisible. We have barely parked before we're asked to produce the official paperwork bearing hard-won stamps from the court in Dohuk that authorizes us to circulate freely. Day after day, we have long discussions with the director of the camp in order to have his authorization to enter, under certain conditions. We assure him that we're not journalists, and we promise to leave at the time he designates.

Each time we go into the camp at Kadia, I am simultaneously impressed and overwhelmed by a strange feeling. Situated in a rocky, uninhabited stretch of land, the camp is surrounded by metal fences and barbed wire. In the distance, I see children playing. Why is this camp so closed off? Why are guards stationed at the entrances? To protect the refugees? From whom? Is it so that the children can run around undisturbed?

The barbed wire serves two purposes simultaneously: to keep outsiders from intruding, but also to keep the people inside from getting out. What never fails to surprise me is that the camp is far from my mental image, gleaned perhaps from the media or maybe just the fruit of my own imagination. I used to picture the camps as windswept, dusty piles of tents jammed into each other with flies everywhere.

Kadia is nothing like that. The trailers are perfectly aligned, the alleys immaculately clean. Inside the dwellings, furnished only with thin mattresses, there isn't a speck of dirt. It all reflects the dignity of the Yazidis, of which the Islamic State has been unable to rob them.

Our faces are lined with fatigue. The day has been draining. Once again, we put on the shoes that we have left outside the trailer in which we've just interviewed a survivor. They have taken on the chalky color of the dust in the camp. From the end of the alley where they've parked their cars, the four bodyguards are observing us, alert to the slightest unexpected movement. Their leader, Toufi, is leaning casually against a trailer a few meters from us. He is relaxed in appearance only. I know that the slightest unforeseen gesture would shake him from his lethargy in a second. One can never be too careful. I nod at him and point my chin at our vehicles: it's time to go. We've finished for the day—or at least I thought so.

Zaher, who has, as usual, been the first to leave to scout out the way, suddenly returns with an odd smile on his face. I look at him inquiringly. "Up there, Lawin is there," he says. I raise my eyebrows. "He got out of a mass grave alive. Would you be interested in his testimony?" The answer is obvious: yes, and it cannot wait until tomorrow. We know from experience that putting something off until tomorrow risks forever being unable to find this crucial witness. Without even lacing up our shoes, which are of no use now, we follow Zaher.

That young man never ceases to surprise me, with his poise and imperturbable good humor. He glides through the camps like a fish in water, always smiling. He goes to meet people with a disconcertingly natural manner, weaves relationships and little by little opens doors to us, finds intermediaries in the camps who will then help us. It's largely thanks to him and his father, who has many contacts in the camps and didn't hesitate to accompany us there the first few times, that we're able to meet witnesses. Not only does Zaher find refugees who've endured the barbarism of ISIS, but also he persuades them to tell us their story. He reassures the families, convinces the parents. From the moment of our arrival, we've become aware of the importance of Zaher's presence, which has been indispensable to the success of our trip. Indeed, on many occasions witnesses would tell us, "We're speaking to you because you're a Yazidi."

"Got out of the mass graves alive"—the expression freezes my blood and instantly transports me to the center of a little town in Crimea, in a gray Soviet building, with Nina, a Jew who had survived the *Einsatzgruppen*.[7] Her husband was preparing soup while she recounted her story. She showed me her nails, permanently ruined. It was by grabbing onto roots that she had managed to claw her way out of the mass grave into which she'd been thrown and buried under dead bodies. She was four years old at the time.

We're walking uphill. It's hard; it seems interminable because of the heat, but to tell the truth I'm in no rush for it to be

---

7   *Einsatzgruppen* translates as "intervention groups." The *Einsatzgruppen* were police units that had been militarized under the Third Reich. They were in charge of killing opponents of the regime, particularly Jews. Between 1940 and 1944, they eiiminated more than 1.5 million people. They orchestrated the first stage of the Holocaust, shooting and gassing in traveling trucks.

over. I'm afraid of what awaits us: the memory of the mass graves of the modern world in the third millennium, a practice as old as the world, renewed for modern use by the perpetrators of genocide in the twenty-first century.

The first thing I see is the smoke from his cigarette. He's standing, leaning against the door of his trailer, skinny and nervous, body arched. Zaher cajoles. The little incandescent stick that Lawin is holding between his yellowed fingers shakes in every direction. He hesitates. I look at him, trying to convey all the empathy I'm able to muster this late in the day. He gestures brusquely to us to come in. We remove our shoes.

He is coiled at the back of his trailer, in the corner, as though he were about to spring. He talks fast and loud, with the voice of a man who has suffered much and knows that something worse is never far away. He's afraid of being recognized: "Please don't show my face!" The interview starts with a burst. He has made up his mind, and he knows exactly what he wants to let us know.

Lawin is twenty-three years old. Like Shvan, he comes from the village of Kojo, which was attacked by ISIS. He specifies right off: "When they arrived, I fought. I had a Russian machine gun, a BKC." But as in all the other areas devastated by the jihadis, the killers disarmed the inhabitants by means of a ruse. They promised that they'd be safe, and that they could come to an understanding if they gave up their weapons. After the men of Kojo surrendered, there began a long series of negotiations between the *mokhtar*, the village chief, and a sheikh of the Islamic State, the object being the Yazidis' conversion to Islam. ISIS demanded immediate renunciation of their faith.

A friend of Lawin's, who until now had been leaning against the door frame, silent and motionless, comes over to us to interrupt the conversation. I hadn't noticed this discreet observer, half-hidden in the shadow. He speaks fast in a loud voice. Taken by surprise, Zaher doesn't have time to translate. Lawin's friend reaches his phone out to Valy, who suddenly understands: "He has taken a picture of the 'negotiations.'" Valy has a hard time believing what he finds on the little luminous screen: seated comfortably around a table on white plastic chairs, two men are talking. The picture shows no trace of animosity. It could just as easily be a completely ordinary meeting, an innocuous conversation. An illusion of civility as backdrop of widespread massacre—the charade is revolting.

Seeing this photograph makes me realize how much genocide has become a fixture of modern times. It has entered our homes, our TV rooms. Snapshots of this genocide, initiated in the comfortable, contemporary setting of a living room, are troubling. Genocide, twenty-first-century style.

On August 15, 2014, following Kojo's refusal to convert, the men of ISIS invaded the village. "In the morning, they came with about eighty cars. They surrounded us and herded us over to the school. They made the women, girls, and children go up to the second floor. The men remained on the ground floor." The killers began by confiscating the men's belongings. They made them turn over their phones and everything they had on their person. One of them walked among the rows, carrying a large sack. Witness the standard criminal procedure: selection, triage, separation of the families, and confiscation of belongings are only the initial steps for the practitioners of genocide. Same method, same actions, same murderous archaic gestures for every mass murder. I force myself to let none of these thoughts show in my expression. I've heard what Lawin is relating so many times in Eastern Europe—but here, in Iraq, it seems different to me. It has just happened, and it's ongoing.

After their last refusal to convert to Islam, the men of Kojo were led out in small groups to the cars that were waiting for them. When he gets to the transporting of the men, Lawin's features suddenly harden; his voice gets cold with hatred and suffering. According to him, the cars took the Yazidis "not very far from the village school." That makes me wonder. I've often studied the digging of the mass graves of the Jews and Roma shot by the Nazis. I know that, in order to make the men of Kojo disappear, the location and the size of the mass grave had to be planned beforehand: the dimensions had to have been calculated according to the volume of the bodies, the hole had to have been dug. That is not something that can be improvised. In Iraq, the soil is very hard, especially in the middle of August, under the burning sun. When executing Jews en masse, the Germans used to send specialists to the area of the projected massacre to calculate the dimensions of the hole to be dug to accommodate the number of people they were planning to kill.

How did the men of ISIS have the time, in the interval between the first and second attacks, to prepare such a site without alerting the townspeople?

Lawin goes on with his story. His voice is dry, his speech choppy, uneven. He's reliving the events, and I admire his courage. "They had already taken away three groups of men.

The fourth time they took me away too. We knew they were going to kill us. They took us to a farm. There were reservoirs for water. They told us to get out of the cars. I knew almost all of the killers."

In a flash, I understand. The executioners in Kojo aren't strangers from far away. Some are Sunni neighbors allied with ISIS! *You can't have genocide without neighbors*, I think. The Kojo region was in no way unfamiliar to them. They knew that the farm had large reservoirs dug into the ground, which explains why the Yazidis didn't attempt to run away after the first attack. They were surrounded by armed neighbors, accomplices of the killers. One never imagines being killed by one's neighbor. Later on, many Yazidis would ask us the same question: "In your opinion, who is ISIS? Only the men in black, or also the neighbors who came to kill or sell us?"

"They told us to stand next to each other in the ditch and raise our hands," continues Lawin. Not surprisingly, one of the murderers took out his cell phone to immortalize the scene. He filmed the Yazidis first standing in the reservoir, then their bullet-torn bodies on the ground, piled on top of each other in what had become a mass grave. Not only do the men of ISIS feel no shame in committing their crimes, they take pride in these atrocities, which they record and transmit over social networks. The cell phone becomes a bloody conveyor of propaganda.

"There were about fifty of us men. They filmed and taunted us, 'If the angel Melek Taus can save you, all he has to do is come now!'" Right up to the end, the killers humiliated the faith of their prey.

Then the cameraman of the moment, who was facing the Yazidis, told his comrades to unload their weapons of war. Five bullets struck Lawin in the back. When all the men of Kojo had fallen, one of the ISIS murderers strode over the ditch to finish off any who were still breathing with a bullet to the head.

I interrupt Lawin: "And you, how did you survive?"

"I tried not to move, but they saw I was still alive. They shot a sixth bullet into my neck. Then they got back into their cars. I heard them rev the engines and leave."

Lawin summoned his last ounce of strength to get out of the ditch. He'd noticed a bulldozer and knew the murderers would soon be rushing back to bury the victims once the massacre was over. He hid in a small room in the farmhouse for more than six hours, until nightfall. "I put dirt on my wounds to stop the bleeding."

While we prepare to leave, Lawin adds one last thing. The man who had shot him in the neck was his own neighbor. He had fished out the cell phone that Lawin had managed to conceal in his pocket. Six days later that same neighbor—the killer—called all of the contacts in Lawin's phone to boast about the crime he'd committed. Proud and eager to spread fear, he repeated to each of Lawin's friends, "I killed the man this phone belonged to."

After fleeing, Lawin hid at the home of a friend. One day, that friend got a call from the killer. On hearing the voice of his torturer, Lawin ran over to the receiver to scream that he wasn't dead and that he'd avenge himself. Startled to hear the voice of his victim, the killer replied simply, "You're alive? So you must have seven lives," and hung up.

Since then, Lawin has become a Peshmerga fighter. He had rejoined his family in the Kadia camp simply to rest between two battles in Sinjar, where he would return again to fight for the lost homeland of his ancestors—a land that these Yazidis, who have nothing left, are fiercely determined to liberate from the criminals who robbed them of everything.

In silence, we head back to the hotel. Valy is moved and troubled, as I can see on his face. Several times during the trip I hear him murmur, "The rage to live . . ."

The rage to live of the Yazidis who have suffered massacre in response to the murderous rage of the ISIS jihadists. The bumps in the road keep time with my thoughts. I try to put it all together, to organize the mass of information received these last few days. Children kidnapped, to be trained and to swell the ranks of the Islamic State. Men murdered because they refuse to convert.

Excerpt from the Interview with Lawin

In which village were you born?
I was born in Kojo.

How did ISIS come to Kojo?
On August 3, 2014, the Peshmerga left, and after that ISIS surrounded the village.

Is Kojo a town or a village?
It's a village.

Is it the only village named Kojo or are there others?
There is only one village named Kojo.

Where were you when the ISIS men arrived?
I was in Kojo with a PKM[8] machine gun.

Were you a Peshmerga?
No, we were defending our village.

What happened next?
Some people from the village fled, about fifteen carsful.

Were you in one of those cars?

No, the first fifteen cars were able to get away. ISIS made the rest turn back. So we hid the weapons since we didn't have a lot of them. They told us to hold up a white flag.

---

8 Lawin is referring to his BKC machine gun, mentioned earlier. The BKC is a clone of the Russian PKM.

And then?
They asked for our weapons. We gave them some of them. We'd hidden the rest of them.

After you had given them some of the weapons, did they lock you up?
We were in the village *mokhtar*'s meeting room. The ISIS soldier told us, "We didn't come here to kill you. We came to apply Islamic law." We didn't have enough weapons to fight.

Who told you that?
Abu P.

And the village chief, what was his name?
Ahmad Jesso.

What language did Abu H. speak?
He spoke Arabic. He was from the region.

Did you think they were going to spare you?
We didn't believe them, but we didn't have any choice. The village was surrounded.

After saying that, what did he say?
Afterward, we met among ourselves. The ISIS cars were still encircling the village. They told us that we had three days to convert to Islam. If not, they were going to kill us.

What happened after that?
Ahmad Jasso told them that we weren't going to convert to Islam. All the men said they weren't going to convert.

And then?
The morning of the fifteenth of August, they came with about eighty cars around the village, and they told us to go into the school at the entrance of the village. It has two stories. They had told the women, the girls, and the children to go up to the second floor, and we men stayed on the ground floor.

And then?
The first thing they said was, "Your phones, money, and gold."

Did they put them into a basket?
They put them into bags.

And then?
After having confiscated everything, they kept asking us to convert to Islam. "Anyone who converts to Islam will be able to get his family and leave here."

And?
We didn't agree to convert to Islam. So they brought in cars and made the villagers get into them.

To take them far from the village?
No, not very far.

Was it an area that Abu H. was familiar with? Did he take them to a particular place?

Yes. He had some land around the village, with a ditch. They took the men there.

Were you taken there?

They took the men there three times. The fourth time they took me, too. They made us get out. We knew they were going to kill us. They took us to a farm. Reservoirs for water had been dug there. They took us there in four cars.

And then?

They told us to get out of the cars. One of them spoke Kurdish, some of them spoke Turkoman. Another spoke in Arabic. I knew all of them except the one from Tal Afar.

And then?

Then they told us to go stand beside one another in the ditch.

Lying down?

No, they said, "Stand up, and put your hands up."

How many of you were there?

About fifty men. They filmed us and said, "If the angel Melek Taus can save you, all he has to do is come."

And then?

The one who was filming asked the other ISIS men to shoot us with their weapons. There were twelve shooters.

Everyone fell?
They shot at us, I was hit by five bullets in my back, and
they stopped. There were some people still alive. One of
the ISIS men shot them in the head with a pistol.

How did you survive?
I tried not to move. They said, "That one, too. He's alive,"
and they shot the sixth bullet into my neck.

And then?
Then they started their cars and left for the village.

Did you see them leave or did you lose consciousness?
I heard them leave. They went to get other men. I'd seen a
bulldozer in the village. I thought they were going to bury
us.

What did you do at that time?
When they left, I got out of the reservoir. I got about 150
meters away, next to an electrical generator. There was
a little room, and I hid in it from one thirty until eight
o'clock in the evening.

And that's how you were able to survive?
Yes. I didn't have a choice. To stop the bleeding, I put dirt
on my wounds.

Did you see the bulldozer arrive?
Yes.

They buried them all?
Yes.

How old was the youngest one?
They were between fifteen and seventy years old.

How many men were killed that day?
They took away three groups of men. We were the fourth group. They shot us. I didn't see anyone move. Maybe they were dead; maybe some of them were injured. They weren't able to get out before the bulldozer got there to bury them. While the ISIS men were shooting us, planes were passing overhead.

Were they ISIS planes?
No, they weren't ISIS planes. ISIS didn't have planes.

Were they Bashar al-Assad's planes?
I don't know. When I looked up, the planes were flying above us. They weren't flying very high.

Who took care of you?
I had to walk around thirty kilometers to the mountain. Six days. Before that, I'd stopped in a village, but they weren't able to take care of me. I had to keep on walking because of the bullets in my back, until I got to the mountain.

How did you make it to the mountain? Who took care of you on the mountain?
It was thanks to God. When I arrived here, they operated on me. They got the bullets out. Afterwards, I wasn't totally cured, but I took a shotgun and left for the mountain.

Did you come to the mountain to fight?
Yes.

With Yazidi militias or Peshmergas?
I went wherever there was fighting.

Were you able to kill some members of ISIS?
There was combat, we were fighting against them, yes. Up till now, no one has helped me. The Kurds said, "Don't go to Europe; we'll make you an officer," but I'm still waiting.

Is your family still under ISIS control?
Yes, my mother, four or five of my sisters-in-law, and six of my brothers.

Nobody has come back?
Yes, some of my sisters-in-law and my sisters.

What are you planning to do? Stay here, go back and fight, or try to go abroad?
I'm not going to leave here. I want to go to Sinjar to avenge myself.

What kind of weapons were you fighting with?
All kinds of weapons.

Are the weapons Russian or American?
Most of them are Russian weapons.

Are the weapons old or new?
They're old.

THE ISLAMIC JUDGE'S WIFE

August 6, 2015—Kadia camp
Trailer D17

A peculiar change has come about. From here on out, we feel more at ease in Kadia than in our hotel rooms. I've gotten used to the camp's rhythm, its schedules, its noises, its odors, the imprint it leaves on our bodies, the white dust that sticks to our skin. The frenzied activity of the mornings; the lethargy of midday, when the sun boils; the scurrying around in the late afternoons, when mealtime approaches and we have to scavenge something to eat from whatever is available. The sound of steps in the sandy alleys and bare feet on the floor of the trailers. The smell of vegetables warming up on the improvised stands. And the smiles that sometimes break through, welcoming smiles that hide stories, each one more tragic than the last.

There are people I've met in the years I've spent traveling abroad whose faces and names have become signposts in my memory, symbols of a country, a stage in my life. Markers of mankind. About thirty-five years ago, I was working in Calcutta in the hospice of Khaligate, which Mother Teresa had set up in the back of the temple of Kali.[9] To get there every day, I had to force my way onto a bus filled to overflowing, grab on, and make my way between people who, for the most part, were there to worship the goddess. One of those countless faces sticks in my memory.

I don't know his name, but I'll never forget that young man, sitting on a little metal bed, in the room at the left of the entrance where men of all ages came to die with dignity. Legs crossed, very straight, very thin, wearing nothing but a *sirwal*, he, too, was awaiting death. One morning, after having made my way through streets crowded with noisy rickshaws and vendors of all sorts, I was tired. I passed in front of his bed. He didn't move. He recognized me, noticed my haggard features, and, seeing my disarray, pronounced these few words: "I will pray for you." In my head, he remains for me the incarnation of Calcutta, of those infinitely poor people who nevertheless opened their hearts to others, including the young Westerner I was at the time.

In Dédougou, where I taught math for several years, Bertha, a tall old woman who sold *dolo*,[10] used to go walking with me for hours in the bush on little dirt roads. On her head, she would carry a heavy, colorful basket filled with food for visiting "the poor." One day we came upon an old blind couple sitting on the ground in front of their miserable little shack,

---

9   In the Hindu religion, Kali is the goddess of preservation, transformation, and destruction.

10 A mild alcohol.

facing a fire that had gone out, with their white dog lying beside them. Berthe sat down and cooked the provisions she had brought on a makeshift grill. Later, while we were praying together out in the abundance of nature, she said to me in her hoarse voice, "When we help the poor, we discover Jesus."

Avine is one of those markers of humanity. Until the day I die, I'll remember her, a symbol of those Yazidis massacred by ISIS, the embodiment of a wounded people, with all its strengths and weaknesses. It took me a long time to understand her, seeing her again and again.

We've already interviewed several young Yazidi girls. I didn't notice her at first. When I enter her trailer, I don't yet know that in our investigation there will be a before—and an after—Avine.

For interviewing women and young girls, we've adopted a special procedure, since they don't want to recount what they have gone through in front of men, with the exception of certain ones who feel they have nothing left to lose. So that day, it is Sebar, a cousin of Zaher and herself a refugee in Belgium, who translates and poses my questions. I hang back as much as possible, trying to be discreet, unnoticeable. It is Sebar whom the victims see when they respond. Sometimes they categorically reject the presence of men in the room, and we have to leave after we've set up the camera. Sebar then continues the investigation alone.

Sitting among the cousins who've gathered around her, Avine seems no different from the others at the beginning of the conversation. Silent and shy, they're all dressed in black, and Avine fits right in. But the cousins quickly point her out: "She knows much, much more than we do." It's only then that I notice her.

Through the veil that snugly covers her entire head, a lock of black hair peeks out, held back with a simple metal barrette. One is immediately drawn to her face. Her features are fine and regular, but frozen into a hardness. Severe and determined, her gestures are precise. This is the face of resistance, a woman whose life has in no way prepared her for her destiny.

Her father was the janitor of the elementary school in Kojo, a school that Avine wasn't fortunate enough to attend. Her mother took care of the home.

When ISIS arrived, Avine and the other young women of the village were violently separated from their families, then locked up, sold, resold, and abused. Facing our camera, Avine becomes the voice of her kidnapped Yazidi sisters, some of whom have never come back. The way she recounts the events confirms my intuition: she didn't give up easily. Her words reveal her permanent resistance against her torturers.

From the very first arrest, she refused to give in. "The ISIS men forced us to give them our money, gold, and telephones. I had my phone and my sister's, and I tried to hold onto them. A man attempted to take them from me, so I threw them off the second floor, through the window, as hard as I could. Because there were lots of pictures in them." Her instinctive reaction helped save her. After the arrest, the jailers often make an inventory of the prisoners' possessions. Their contents may help determine the punishment, particularly if they find photos of Iraqi soldiers or Peshmergas.

The photos can also help ISIS determine whether there are family members who remain in hiding.

Avine was sold several times in ISIS slave markets. In one particular instance, she was locked up in a house whose inhabitants, Shiites, had been murdered, in a village whose name meant nothing to me at the time. That is standard practice: often ISIS slave merchants buy a large number of women and girls, whom they gather in a place they have under their control while waiting for buyers. While they are monitored closely, the captives can circulate "freely."

In the Shiite house Avine found weapons: "There were Kalashnikovs, pistols, and BKCs [a machine gun made in the Czech Republic]." I listen carefully to her. Once again, her tale surprises me: "We stayed for two months and two weeks in that house. Suddenly, the ISIS men came and searched it. My sister and I had hidden twenty-some weapons." Not only had this girl, who could neither read nor write, learned to recognize these weapons of war, but even more surprising, she had instinctively buried them so they wouldn't be discovered by ISIS during an inspection, which most certainly saved her life as well as those of the other women imprisoned with her.

Avine's story reminds me, in a way, of my mother's, when the Germans came to our farm in Villegaudin: tipped off by some neighbors, the Germans were looking for partisans that my grandmother was suspected of hiding. They went through all the rooms and found some weapons left in the hay in the barn. They ransacked the house and threatened to shoot all the men in the neighborhood. Like Avine, my grandmother hadn't gone to school, but she had learned how to resist.

Avine was next bought by one Jassim Abu M., from Syria, a "wholesaler" who acquired groups of young women and then sold them "by the piece." I was immediately reminded of certain traders in my home area of Bresse, who used to come to our little stable to buy livestock. But those livestock traders didn't mistreat the cows. They were kinder to the animals than the men of ISIS were to their Yazidi slaves. More than religion, what interested Jassim Abu M. was the money he got from trafficking human beings. "He bought the three of us, my neighbor, a girl from Solakh (an Iraqi village not far from Mount Sinjar), and me from the Shiite house. He then sold me for $4,000." Although she didn't show it, I could tell how humiliating it was for Avine to reveal her "market value" for ISIS.

After a certain amount of time, all the prisoners, whoever they were, couldn't help measuring themselves in terms of the values of their torturers. The men of ISIS know this. Selling a Yazidi woman slave cheaply is a way to debase her. It even happens sometimes that in order to humiliate the women even further, their owners will give them away to another ISIS man, letting them know that they are worth nothing at all.

I don't know whether the laws of the radical Islam preached by ISIS regard the sex-slave trade purely in terms of profitability, but plenty of the accounts we have heard seemed to indicate that they do. Within the ranks of the organization, many swear allegiance as much to money as to Islamist ideology. There is no trifling where money is concerned.

Throughout the interviews, the accounts piled up. The slave trade can extend to very young children: one mother tells us that she saw a little seven-year-old girl torn away from her mother, who was herself a prisoner. She was raped by five men, then sold again before dying in the following days. Girls and married women may be purchased at any time. Often a sheikh of the Islamic State goes to a prison accompanied by ISIS fighters, to whom he offers a female slave as a gift.

The men of ISIS feel they have the unlimited right to purchase and rape of Yazidi females. Among them, those who run prisons have the reputation of being especially barbaric. In order to humiliate women who were over forty, one of these men would give the women to soldiers who were thirteen years old. They were all raped by teenagers in rooms adjacent to the cells, within earshot of their own children and their equally unfortunate companions in suffering.

Suddenly, Avine's voice wavers, her expression weakens. Her eyes, unmoving, stare off into space; her face hardens. She appears to be hesitating, searching for words. Then, stone-faced, she describes the rape of her young cousin, who had been bought by an emir.

"Two men held her hands, two others her feet. They gave her an injection to anesthetize her. Afterwards, she did not realize that she had lost her virginity. She was too exhausted; they had thrown a blanket over her and locked her in the room."

I'm disgusted, but I force myself as much as possible not to show it. It's so hard to stay calm when anger burns inside you! Rape under anesthesia. Why? Why call in the local medical corps to facilitate a rape, eliminating the least possibility for the victim to resist? "That very day, the day of the rape, the emir sold her to another man, who raped her, too. That one kept her for eight months, and then he sold her."

Sex and money. The men of ISIS never ignore profit or pleasure, whether stolen or taken by force. Financial possession and rape are the two sides of a single form of savagery. But why did they anesthetize the young woman, why had they alleviated the pain in some way? The use of drugs to make captive women docile is a common practice that other witnesses will mention. ISIS and doping—clearly a thriving enterprise.

Once again, it is by way of my memories and a terrible analogy that I fully understand the horror of the system put in place by the Islamic State. When I was young, I worked in a poultry slaughterhouse in Chalon-sur-Saône. It was strictly forbidden to strike the animals, first of all because my grandfather was against unnecessary violence, but also because the slightest mark on the skin of the animal would have diminished its value and compromised its sale. That unfortunate association, between a relatively benign childhood memory and the events related by Avine, left the taste of ashes in my mouth.

And so, certain slave dealers insist on being the first to rape the girls they buy in order to leave a mark they consider indelible, possessing them physically in a way that money cannot do or undo, before passing them on to someone else. But since they also want to sell them as quickly as possible and for the highest price, avoiding injuries and signs of mistreatment is essential. By keeping the young girls from fighting back, anesthesia makes the rape invisible. Even the victim herself has no conscious memory of the act.

By her way of speaking, directly but modestly, I understand that in recounting the suffering endured by the other girls, Avine is also describing her own.

Avine's new owner was named Abu J. He was a young Saudi from a prominent family, which he had left to join the Islamic State. On several occasions, she heard him having stormy conversations with the relatives who had remained in Saudi Arabia.

Abu J. was adamant about the virginity of the girl he was buying, so before finalizing the transaction he had Avine taken to the hospital in Raqqa, where a female doctor verified that she was still a virgin. With this "formality" done, she was judged worthy of her new master and taken to him. The fact that Avine received relatively light treatment by her jailers is evidence of their greed and their Machiavellian cunning. Since she's young and pretty, they knew that she could be of interest to a rich buyer, so keeping her intact increased her value. Abu J. was all too aware of the unfortunate propensity of the slave-dealing wholesalers to rape girls they were offering for resale.

Upon her return to Abu J.'s house, she kept resisting: "Every night he would come to see me and insist that I be with him. Every night I said no. So he said, 'Like it or not, if you keep this up, I am going to force you!'" A week and a half later, tired of the obstinacy of this girl who was spurning him, he carried out his threat. Accompanied by three friends, he forced her once more to go to the hospital in

Raqqa. A doctor verified Avine's virginity, and then she was raped under anesthesia by her owner. She remained chained to her bed for several days.

Abu J. took her to see her captive cousins on a regular basis. This surprised me, since the only apparent motive was to make Avine happy. A single note of humanity sounding in the ferocious cacophony of ISIS machinations. A man visibly wishing to please a woman. But one day, one of the cousins tried to run away. "They beat my cousin. They tore out her hair. At the back of her skull you could see her skin. Her whole body was black and blue from being beaten with a cable." That was the last time Avine saw her. After that escape attempt, Abu J. put an end to the visits and cut off all remaining ties to her family and her Yazidi past. For the young woman, this was the point of no return: "When they arrested us, I was with my family. I was afraid. But when I found myself alone, separated from my people, I was no longer afraid of anything. I had to remain strong. I was no longer even afraid that Abu J. would kill me."

The interview could have ended there, but some premonition pushes me on. We need to take a break. My team can't take it anymore. After having heard several witnesses today, we're at the end of our rope. I decide to walk around a little outside to stretch my legs. I have trouble getting up, and I am not the only one. We're not used to sitting on the ground for long periods of time.

The sun gradually sets. In front of the trailers, the families are preparing their evening meal. Some things never change: stomachs growling from hunger at a certain time of day and stubborn attempts to recreate a homey atmosphere, maintaining habits as a way of keeping some continuity, recapturing the tastes and smells of a daily routine now lost to them. I walk alone, or rather accompanied only by my bodyguards, in the rock-filled white alley.

Away from the rest of the team, I try to lift my spirits. I look up at the sky. In my head, I keep hearing Avine's words over and over. I'm sure there's something important I'm missing, something her story has given us a glimpse of but that we're not being quick enough to catch.

A few minutes later I climb the stairs to the trailer entrance. "Let's keep going."

To conduct the interviews and collect usable testimony that will constitute evidence of the crimes that have been committed, we've developed a protocol: In the first part of the interview, we have the witnesses tell their stories, guided by our questions. In the second part, we show them about a hundred photographs, kept in a large orange binder. These photos come from propaganda videos or ISIS members' posts on social media. We don't interfere. The witnesses are free to rummage through the binder and react when an image reminds them of something. Sometimes a whole chunk of memory is jogged this way, or else a photo sets off the story of an event the witness hadn't thought worth mentioning because it was so much a part of his or her daily life.

Avine turns the pages attentively. Suddenly, she cries, "I was there!" I lean forward to see the photo she is pointing at. It's the one showing the execution of the Jordanian Muath

Al-Kasasbeh, who was captured by ISIS and burned alive. "I was there! To the left of the iron cage." Instantly, my brain, tired from the long day, wakes up. Just as, in math, the entire hypothesis can suddenly shift, Avine's exclamation opens up a new range of possibilities. If she was present that day, what else might she have seen that she's forgetting to tell us? I know that a part of the population of Raqqa went to watch the pilot burn, but the presence of a Yazidi woman slave is unexpected. I don't believe in single exceptions. If something is true in one place, it is worth asking whether it might be true somewhere else. I want to check whether Avine had other opportunities to attend important events, in spite of her slave status.

I ask her, "You were there? You weren't locked up that day?"

"Abu J., the man who had bought me, never left me alone in the house. He was too afraid I would run away. So he took me along wherever he went."

If she's telling the truth, it's very likely that she knows more about her owner than I thought. Right away I ask her for details on her movements: did they travel in convoys? The question might seem incongruous, but the reason I ask is to determine Abu J.'s stature.

"There were protective vehicles. We always rode in convoys of five cars, one in front and three behind. If planes were bombing, they left the vehicles and went to hide in the fields."

So Avine's owner obviously appears to be an important member of the Islamic State, much more than a simple fighter. With Abu J., the young woman went to Aleppo, Tell

Abyad, Suluk, al-Thawrah, Husaybah, Baghdad, Ramadi. Among them, I recognize, of course, the names of the cities most recently conquered by the Islamic State. One after the other, Valy unfolds the road maps of Iraq and Syria that we bought in France before leaving, in order to track the travels of Abu J. The distances traveled are substantial, sometimes hundreds of kilometers. With a yellow marker, Valy highlights on the map each of the localities mentioned, so we're better able to understand the topography of Avine's story. Seeing us do this, she comments, "Abu J. visited all the areas that have fallen under the control of the Islamic State."

Avine then detailed Abu J.'s schedule. He would leave Raqqa every day at the prescribed hour, driving his jeep, and he would come back fairly late at night. One destination surprises me: Baghdad, the capital of Iraq, wasn't conquered by ISIS. What did he do there? "He was transporting weapons," replied the young woman. And the rest of the time? "He often visited the prisons, especially the one at Raqqa."

Little by little, Avine reveals to us the "secrets of ISIS," to use Abu J.'s expression. She explains slowly, following her own rhythm or perhaps ours, trying to figure out our limits and determining what we can take in and understand.

First she retraces her steps at Abu J.'s side within the prison at Raqqa. She seems to be walking there again—her memories taking her back. Like a former hostage recalling the least details of the cell that had become her universe, she describes minutely, one by one, all the places she went. "There is a large corridor; we went down fifteen steps, then a corridor of about twenty meters long that leads directly to a door with bars, then another door behind which the prisoners are kept. Two guards are at every door and next to the stair-ways." I listen attentively. The geography is beginning to become clearer. I understand—or rather I force myself to accept the understanding—that if the guards allowed her to move around freely at Abu J.'s side, it's because they considered her to be not a Yazidi slave belonging to him, but rather his wife. Meanwhile, dressed in her *niqab* like an ISIS woman, encased in the black-cloth prison that both enclosed and protected her, Avine continued to live like a prisoner, noticing everything, counting the meters, recalling the color of the walls in order to survive, with the hope of running away and someday perhaps bearing witness.

Avine's attitude, gestures, and words remind me of those of the Maranos, Jews forcibly converted under the Inquisition in Spain. Some of them hung hams from their windows to make the Christians outside think they were of the same faith. But within the shelter of their homes, they continued praying the Sh'ma Yisrael.[11]

Abu J. used to go to the Raqqa prison to oversee torture sessions. He would enter the cells, choose the prisoner he was going to interrogate, and then, sitting on a chair with Avine at his side, tell his men which tortures to apply. She had to remain seated, without moving, and watch without reacting, at least in appearance. "At first, I was afraid. Then, since I was seeing tortures every day, I got used to it. If I cried, he would hit me with electric cables and hoses."

---

11 The Sh'ma, consisting of three excerpts from the Torah, is the main text of Jewish liturgy.

I wonder: She never mentions the cries and screams of the torture victims, as though the beatings doled out by her "owner" and her will to survive had gradually made her deaf to their cries. When one has to do so much just to stay alive, the suffering of others can become inaudible.

Avine reminds me of my friend Shlomo Venezia, who was forced to work in the gas chambers of the extermination camp at Birkenau. He saw thousands of men, women, and children who were to die, asphyxiated, as soon as the doors closed and the Zyklon B gas was released. When the gassing and the ventilation were finished, along with his comrades in misfortune, he had to open the doors. Sometimes he would find a baby still alive in its mother's arms—a baby that, like everyone else, was destined to die.

While Avine is describing in detail the tortures organized by her owner, I think about the expression she used a few minutes ago: "He was too afraid that I would run away." These words aren't insignificant. Why would an emir of the Islamic State be so afraid that a slave would escape that he would never leave her alone at home? If need be, he could have found himself another slave—unless he felt a certain attachment to her, even affection, and held out some hope that one day those feelings would be reciprocated, since having her with him wherever he went meant he risked revealing many secrets.

Abu J. forbade Avine to betray any sign that she was a prisoner, a slave. He wanted to toughen her up, make her behave like a woman of the Islamic State. She pretended to obey him in order to avoid death, and, in the eyes of the others, she had become the wife of an Islamist judge in the organization. "Yes, he considered me his wife. He would tell me his secrets and tell me repeatedly that he would never leave me." With difficulty, she explains that every morning she had to strap an explosive belt under her clothes. "If anyone attacks us, we'll blow ourselves up together," he used to tell her. Avine didn't try to deceive Abu J. She never led him to think she was resigned. "He thought I would never succeed in escaping."

Avine witnessed so many torture sessions that she recounts them with no emotion. Abu J. filmed all of them with his phone. The victims were, from what he said, for the most part prisoners who refused to convert to Islam—Peshmergas or members of the Free Syrian Army—and thus, as far as he was concerned, "infidels." "Sometimes he asked them to join ISIS," she relates.

The reason for imprisonment and torture could nevertheless be much more banal: having smoked a cigarette, for example. All the interrogations were carefully recorded in registries. The main instrument was electricity, which the emirs' henchmen applied to the soles of the feet, sometimes for almost two hours, after having beaten the prisoner.

Once the interrogation was over, Abu J. would decide on the punishment. When the prisoner was condemned to death, he was dressed in orange and then executed, usually outside the prison. This is the first time I'm questioning at such length a witness who has attended recent torture sessions.

Abu J. would drive his car up to the site of the execution and give the order with a wave of the hand. Most of the time

Avine remained in the car and observed, shielded within her cloth prison. At the Halab prison, she witnessed large numbers of beheadings: "One time fifteen, one time thirty-five, one time fifty."

These aren't just numbers, they're murders. A sick feeling overwhelms me. It's too much. I get up and tell Valy to take over. I can't take any more. I know my limits and how important it is to respect them.

I go outside but can't help listening to the rest of the account: "It was well-organized, like in a movie. The killers laid them down on their bellies and put their [severed] heads on their backs." Like the Ukrainians who witnessed the killings of their Jewish neighbors, she reveals the unvarnished truth without flinching. She goes on recounting more and more atrocities committed before her eyes as if it were a movie. I think, although I'm not sure of this, that it's a defense mechanism. She simply cannot do otherwise. The overload of horrors witnessed by Avine has ended up removing her from an unbearable reality.

Valy is the next to leave the trailer, pale and visibly exhausted. During the return trip to the hotel, nobody says a word. We don't even talk during the meal. I have trouble falling asleep. I'm haunted by the woman's face; her testimony torments me. Once more, I realize that human beings at times have no choice other than to get used to the very worst.

Survival in extreme situations sometimes takes on disturbing forms that trouble the consciences of those who have been spared. Often people who are safely looking on from the outside try to understand the situation; they frame it in inapplicable categories and end up passing judgment. It is the classic refrain: "If I had been alive at the time of World War II, I would have joined the Resistance." Nothing is less certain, and the hundreds of millions of people who were content to do nothing, to see nothing, weren't necessarily bad people.

Black and white—this way of looking at life prevails only for people who haven't known continual horror. The world isn't Manichean. There aren't heroes on one side and cowards and villains on the other, but men and women who, in the face of evil, make do as best they can to secure their daily existence. Furthermore, acts of resistance against the enemy aren't necessarily spectacular. For Avine, escaping, trying to get her life back together, and bearing witness are acts of resistance. Stubbornly rejecting the traces of indulgence that sometimes creep into her voice when she speaks of Abu J., she is eliminating her oppressor.

Abu J.'s attitude toward the young woman is instructive about the way the Islamic State looks at the Yazidis. Racism in combination with the certainty of absolute truth leads to subjugation of the other, starting with women, who are part of the spoils of war. The jihadists believe themselves to be all-powerful. They can turn all females into sex slaves, or they can take them as wives. Women remain, for them, merchandise to be bought, with minds to brainwash, bodies to defile, and souls to be molded, even to the point of making them combatants. Abu J. seems to me a bit like an Islamist Pygmalion doing his best to transform Avine into the perfect jihadist wife, from nonbeliever to fervent fundamentalist, because he liked her. Insanely radical, he must have believed that the finest gift he could give his slave was to turn her into a copy of himself. In this story, religion is no more than the backdrop. What counts is the intention of the emir, who is able to reach an accommodation with Sharia to the point of treating a *kafir* as if she were a wife.

Months later, we see Avine again. Time has brought her some measure of peace. Slowly, she seems to have more or less returned to her life. She remains forever scarred but more determined than ever.

On the occasion of this new meeting, she tells us about her escape. Abu J. had left for the funeral of some ISIS fighters. In an internet café, she contacted a smuggler whose number she knew. They set up a meeting time, and a car came to pick her up, along with her cousin. She had also tried to bring two of her nephews with her—aged ten and fourteen. They refused; they wanted remain with ISIS. The brainwashing had worked.

"We didn't tell them what day we were leaving," she added.

"Why?" I asked, surprised.

"Because they would have killed us. They had joined ISIS."

I signal to Oscar to shut off the camera, but Valy wants to ask a final question, the one thing that, in all those long hours of interviewing her, none of us had dared to bring up: "Wait. While you were watching the torture sessions, the beheadings, what did you feel?" Avine looks up, her eyes empty: "I didn't feel anything. I also was part of ISIS."

I remain convinced that Avine is a young woman who resisted right up to the end, who tried to remain a Yazidi beneath the ISIS trappings piled on her. But the beatings, the screams of the torture victims that she heard day after day, the heads cut off—horror had taken her to the outer limits of what it means to be human. Confronted with the unbearable, ceasing to think, becoming at times the creature that her owner wished her to be had been her last defense against annihilation.

Excerpt from Interview with Avine

Were some prisoners punished in front of you?
Yes. Wherever he went, he took me with him.

What did they do to them at the Halab prison?
If someone smoked, they took him to that prison, and Abu
J. decided what type of punishment he would get—electric
cables, chains . . .

**And did the punishment take place in the prison or
outside?**
They took them into a room set aside especially for torture.

Was it men or women who got tortured?
Men.

What nationality were the people who got tortured?
It was a mix. I don't know what countries they were from.

Were the men tied up?
Yes, their hands were tied behind their backs.

Children, too?
From eighteen on.

**And did Abu J. watch during the torture sessions, or
did he wait until they were finished?**
He stayed seated. There were six or seven men with them.
He gave the orders.

And you were sitting next to him?
Yes.

Which kind of torture was used the most? Beatings, electricity?
Electricity was used often, but they hit them a lot too.

For the electricity, did they use cables or car batteries?
They took cables and put them under the feet for an hour or an hour and a half.

Were those the only punishments, or were there also interrogations?
They interrogated them too. They asked, "Why are you refusing to join ISIS?" Or else sometimes it was because they had been smoking.

And so, when they took the man away, the punishment had already been decided on? Or was it Abu J. who decided on it?
It was after he had interrogated him. Whether the prisoner admitted or not, it was then that he decided.

What was the worst punishment that was decided on there?
Death.

If it was death, did they kill him right away?
No, first they dressed him in orange clothing.

Did they put the orange clothing on him in the prison?
Yes, they would dress him in orange before taking him some place to decapitate him.

And did Abu J. stay at the prison? Or did he go with the others for the beheadings?
He would go with them. He was the one who gave the order.

During the beheadings, would he watch from the car, or did he get out?
I stayed in the car. He went out, but he didn't do the beheading.

Was the one who cut off the heads always masked?
Yes, and all the others had their faces covered.

Except for him?
Yes, he didn't cover his face.

Was there someone in charge who ordered the beheadings?
Yes, it was the man who was with me. He was the one who gave the order, and they all did the beheadings together.

Was it well organized?
Yes, it was well organized, like in a movie.

And what did they do with the heads?
They laid the bodies down on their bellies and placed the heads on the backs.

And when the people were dead, did they recover the orange outfits?
No, they left them.

You often say that you knew the secrets of ISIS. In your opinion, what is the biggest secret you knew and that the organization didn't want you to reveal?
The prisons. They didn't want anyone to know about them.

What did they want to keep secret, their location or the tortures?
The locations of the prisons and the places where there were Yazidi men.

Were they prisoners? Or were they killed?
They were prisoners. They were the young ones, the children.

Did you also go with Abu J. into the places where they were training children?
Yes, when the planes weren't passing. It was in large houses and schools. But when the planes were bombing, they moved to a different place. They took them into another town that was safer.

How many children were there per center?
Around 1,500 Yazidi children.

Were the children you saw all trained in the same way? Or were certain of them trained to shoot guns or plant bombs?
They trained them to read the Koran. As soon as a boy grew up, they took him to fight. The little ones guarded the checkpoints.

We've already interviewed certain children who seem to have been trained to plant bombs. Were there children specially trained to plant bombs?
Yes, they were. Everyone had his work. For example, they made the big ones become fighters, younger ones were put on the checkpoints, and the little ones were in charge of loading bullets, cleaning the weapons, and even making the bomb material.

And for carrying the bombs, was it the little ones, the ones in the middle, or the big ones?
Up to the age of eleven.

And those who prepared the bomb materials, how old were they?
Nine, ten years old.

How many children prepared the bombs?
Many. They weren't just Yazidi children. There were Muslims too.

Did you see the places where they prepared the explosive belts?
Yes, and the man I was with had an explosive belt.

Why? In case he got arrested?
He used to say, "If someday I'm arrested, I'll blow myself up."

You said you went to the execution of the Jordanian man, which was public. Did you see other public executions? Beheadings, for example, where there would have been lots of people?
Yes, I saw lots of executions. Three times big ones, other times little ones.

How were you able to deal with all that?
At the beginning I was afraid, but since I was seeing them every day, I got used to it. And if I cried, he would hit me.

Abu J. hit you?
Yes, with electrical cables and hoses.

Did you see any women being punished?
No.

You saw people sentenced to death, beheadings, and people being burned. Were there any others?
Some were shot with heavy weapons.

Did you see large-scale firing squads?
It was like the beheadings. There was somebody behind, and he would do the shooting.

What is the biggest official firing-squad execution you saw?
Lots of them, sometimes a hundred or a hundred fifty. In Halab, they killed one hundred fifty.

And were there also one hundred fifty shooters?
Yes.

Was it Abu J. who had given the order?
He and his friends.

Did he tell you in advance that you were going to see that?
No. He took me along with him so that I would see how Yazidis were punished and stop talking about my family.

Did he think that in the end you would no longer think of your family and that you would stay with him forever?
Yes.

In your opinion, since you left, do you think he's still in love with you?
Yes, I think so.

Do you think he took you first as a slave and then all of a sudden he fell in love with you and wanted to keep you forever?

When he bought me, he took me as a *sabya*,[12] but afterwards I didn't become a servant. I cooked just for him and me.

As a wife, then?

Yes.

Did he tell you he wanted to have children with you?

Yes, he said that, but I didn't agree.

Now, in your sleep, do you still see him? Is he still in your head?

No, I think back on the beheadings and the murders.

Did he ever sell you to someone else for a day or two?

No.

Do you think you are the only one in that situation, or were there other ISIS men who ended up falling in love with a girl they'd bought?

I think there were others.

And if someday he's brought to justice, what would you like to have done to him?

The worst punishment in the world.

---

12 A sex slave.

Do you think he has found another woman?
He said he was going to marry a Muslim woman.

When you were with him, did he want to take another wife?
Yes, he used to say he was going to take a Muslim wife too.

Did he already have children with someone?
No. He had a wife in Saudi Arabia. When he got to Syria to join the Islamic State, he'd been married for six months.

What did he do before joining ISIS? Did he have a profession?
He was a teacher.

A teacher of children or a specialized teacher?
He didn't say.

Did he get mail from Saudi Arabia?
He used to talk to his wife on the phone.

What was your house like? Tall, small, big?
It was a big house with three floors.

Was it just the two of you in the house?
Yes, but with guards.

Did you have any female servants, since you were like a wife?

No, I did the cooking myself. He used to eat in a restaurant. On the ground floor were the guards.

So he never ate with you. Did he always eat at the restaurant?

Yes, he ate at the restaurant. He didn't want anyone to know that I was a Yazidi, other than the Yazidis who came to visit me.

When you went out, did you wear makeup or was that *haram* [forbidden]?

It was *haram*. There were some who wanted their wives to do it, but he never did.

Did he say they were going to attack Baghdad?

Yes, every day he mentioned the places they had attacked.

Did those ISIS men talk only about Iraq and Syria, or did they also mention Tunisia or Afghanistan?

They said they were going to be going into Saudi Arabia, Tunisia, Turkey, and Afghanistan.

Did they get phone calls coming from those countries?

A month before I ran away, they called two fourteen-year-old boys in Turkey to get them to join the Islamic State.

Were they Turkish, or were they boys who had arrived after having crossed through Turkey?
They were Syrians who had fled with their families and taken refuge in Turkey. They spoke to them in secret. They wanted to join ISIS.

Did you visit a place where there were young people from Europe or America or elsewhere, who didn't know how to fight but were going to be trained to be fighters?
Yes, I already visited some. There were boys like the fourteen-year-olds who wanted to join ISIS. I saw a Chinese boy who killed two Peshmergas.

How old was that boy?
Eleven.

Were those boys used in public beheadings?
No, they had administrative duties as guards. They weren't yet old enough to fight.

So those children who came from abroad were more likely to have administrative jobs?
Yes, until they learned to fight and handle weapons.

Among themselves, did those boys speak in Arabic or the language of their country?
[The witness misunderstood the question.] They spoke Arabic with the boys who knew Arabic, and if they didn't

know Arabic, they spoke to them in the language of their country.

Did you see any Australians?
Yes, they came from all over, but mostly from Saudi Arabia.

Which big cities in Syria did you go to?
Raqqa is the biggest city.

And the farthest one?
Mosul. He was visiting his leader, and he left me waiting in a hotel room.

In ISIS territory, did the hotels continue to function normally?
Yes, those that supported ISIS kept on working, and the others had left.

In Mosul, is auto traffic normal, or is there almost no one there since the city has been in ISIS hands?
The people of the other regions can no longer enter the city the way they used to. The people who support ISIS keep on conducting business, and the others have left the city. Their businesses have been taken over by ISIS.

Did you go to Mosul when you were free, before ISIS arrived?
Yes, I went there several times with the whole family.

When you came back with him, had the city changed a lot?
Yes, it was not like it used to be. Everything had changed: before, the people were free; they no longer are. Now everything is controlled by ISIS.

Were the same policemen there or had they been replaced?
The Islamic State replaced the policemen.

Was Abu J. an ISIS chief or chieftain?
They called him the sheikh. An important man is called a sheikh or a *wali*.

Was he a fighter also?
Chief and fighter at the same time, since everyone had to fight.

When you went somewhere, if someone asked you whether you were a fighter, did you have to answer that you were with them?
Yes, he would put a weapon on my shoulder and an explosive belt. He used to tell me that, if the enemy entered Raqqa, I was to defend him if he needed it. He forced me.

When you went out with him, did you see other men with their fighter wives?
Yes, that was normal. The women had weapons, too, and explosive belts, and they carried their weapons even when they went to the market.

Had he given you an important name to show that you were an important fighter with him?
Yes, he didn't say I was a *sabya*. He said I was his wife.

Do you think, in the end, he forgot you were a Yazidi and that for him you had become a fighter?
Yes. If I hadn't run away, he would never have let me leave. He used to tell me he wouldn't sell me even if someone gave him a lot of money.

Do you think he's still alive?
I don't think so. I don't know.

Did he take risks in combat?
Yes, he took lots of risks. He constantly repeated that he was going to die. I told myself that since he always said that, he wasn't going to die.

Do you realize how incredible your story is, that you were able to fool him into thinking you had become a fighter?
That was what I intended to do. I made him believe that I was a fighter to understand why they behaved the way they did with the Yazidis. I was with him for almost a year, and I wasn't able to contact my family.

Did he tell his family in Saudi Arabia that he had found a woman and that he had gotten married?
No, he didn't speak with his family; he spoke only to his wife.

In your opinion, did he come from a high-ranking family in Saudi Arabia?

Yes, they were important in their country. His brothers used to say to him: "If they catch you, they will decapitate you."

NOT PRETTY ENOUGH

August 8, 2015—Kadia camp

The days go by, all seeming pretty much the same. Mornings going to the camps, returning late, our ears filled with stories of atrocities, our hearts and minds racked by the suffering of these men and women we're growing attached to. The scorching sun, tireless and never late for the rendezvous as we labor on in the stifling heat.

The car slows down. Zaher and Subhi, the head of our security team, roll down their windows to call to some old men wearing red-and-white turbans. A gust of suffocating dry heat invades the car.

What's going on?" I ask.

"We're looking for a family," replies Zaher.

The motor growls, the dust swirls again, and we drive up to Trailer D35, second alley on the left at the top.

Conducting interviews in the trailers is bothering me more and more. I know that inside I'll find a whole family sitting there, fifteen people sometimes, whom I'll have to ask to leave, in spite of the heat, because a survivor, most likely a woman, can't relate the humiliations she has been subjected to in front of her family. On top of the horror, there would be added shame and maybe expulsion. The summer heat magnifies my discomfort. The family always agrees to find another place to shelter from the sun during the interview, all of them aware of the necessity for their absence so that their daughter, their son, or their grandmother can bear witness, and all convinced of the absolute necessity of this testimony.

Zaher, who is leading the group, points out a young girl leaning against the door frame: "That's her!" She's small, with large, dark eyes, black hair tied back, and a strikingly hard face that looks almost as if it were carved out of stone. Her skin bears the scars of a childhood spent outdoors under the punishing sky of Iraq, but I also discern the signs of unspeakable pain. The rest of the family sits in the little bit of shade provided by the trailer beneath a sun that's already high in the sky. Zaher loses his composure, which is rare, and whispers, "There's no electricity!" That happens often. No electricity, no ventilation, 120 degrees in the trailer. Up till now, we've been pretty much spared this problem, which is apparently frequent in such remote places. The refugee camps aren't as well equipped as the ISIS training camps.

Our guards signal us not to stay out in the broiling sun but to get into our air-conditioned cars. Recalling my three years in Burkina Faso, in what was known at the time as Upper Volta, I call out to Zaher and Valy: "We have to find a generator. I'm sure there must be a family that owns one. Ask them if they'll agree to rent it to us. And don't forget the gas."

Valy eyes me skeptically but does as I say. An hour later, the two come back carrying an old yellow generator, which doesn't want to start. Finally, on the hundredth try, we hear the hum of the motor and enter the trailer.

Her name is Payman. For some reason that I can't explain, I find her intimidating. She seems not to be any particular age, but I'd say she's over twenty-five. Her body, her features, the way she sits—her whole being cries out the mistreatment she has endured. I expect the worst.

Sitting across from us, she speaks first of her childhood, her life in the village and at school, a happy existence before the men of ISIS arrived. Six brothers and sisters, the father a soldier in the Iraqi army who used to go "far away" for ten days, then come back home. Suddenly, I start shuddering. In one little sentence, she has just given away her age. She's fifteen years old. What kind of hellish life could have made her look ten years older?

In her own words, she reconstructs the arrival of the men of ISIS. She speaks clearly, without hesitating, detailing the sequence of events that upended her life. Like Lawin, she says the Islamists began by demanding that the entire village convert to Islam. As if to prove they were serious, they designated the location of the future mosque. I've already met many survivors from Kojo, but Payman is the first to describe this point and the first to mention one crucial detail: the men of ISIS arrived with six or seven cloth sacks, all identical, in which the Yazidis were supposed to deposit their most valuable belongings—proof that the looting is organized and planned ahead of time, institutionalized. "We had to give up the seven phones our family owned!" This last remark makes me smile inside—the regret of a child from a village that's both remote and connected to the modern world. She is indeed a twenty-first-century fifteen-year-old. For my part, I couldn't say how many phones my brother's family has.

The villagers' refusal to cooperate set off the deadly, implacably cruel sequence of events: the men were arrested; the young girls, including Payman, were dragged away from their families and carried off like animals to Suluk, then Mosul, and finally Raqqa. Her account is a bit confused, which doesn't surprise me. She's a teenager who had never left the rural setting of her childhood. How could she be expected to remember all the stages of her journey to hell?

The time in prison, on the other hand, is etched in her memory: one day in a mosque in Mosul, fourteen days in Raqqa in what was formerly a tourist venue but is now populated almost entirely by young girls. In Mosul, a female ISIS doctor verified that they were virgins. Disgusted, I'm reminded of the way African slaves were treated. The body becomes merchandise to be prodded, weighed, verified. The information thus gathered serves as a basis for calculating the market value. I hazard a question: "How old was the youngest girl with you?" Without hesitation she answers, "Twelve."

Like a vase filled so full it overturns and breaks, she pours out the worst horrors. Emirs filed into the house in Raqqa, where she was being held prisoner, to select the prettiest girls. They looked over the faces and bodies. I assume it was during this kind of visit that Abu J. bought Avine. Payman's face darkens, hardens. They didn't choose her. Payman, the girl with jet-black hair, had not only endured the affront of being reduced to slavery but also been judged to be not pretty enough. The bitterness I read in her eyes reminds me of Zana, the young would-be sniper. The humiliation of not even meeting the standards of one's executioners! "Not pretty enough"—that verdict was to lead Payman into the depths of horror, for she was destined not for the emirs and the *walis* but for the common military rabble of ISIS.

As a man, I feel uncomfortable knowing that it was a bunch of men, or rather males, who knowingly committed this barbaric violence. I decide to step back and let Sebar conduct the rest of the interview.

A dozen pretty girls were selected by the "princes." Along with the remaining girls, Payman was given a *niqab* and a colored scarf. For the two weeks that followed, at any hour of the day or night, men would come into the room where they were detained, uncover the faces, and buy one, two, or three girls. These transactions were carried out in public. The men would turn up with money, and the jailers would write out a receipt and note the address where the girl who had been purchased was going to be locked up by her new owner.

Slavery under ISIS is nothing less than a totalitarian bureaucracy, governed by laws, codified, supervised. Everything is recorded, and a human being can, without the least scruple, become a commodity to be bought and sold. In that sense, the Islamic State echoes Nazi ideology. In Nazi

Germany, young Aryans held the power of life and death over those they had detached from the human race. The Islam of ISIS is thus simultaneously a theory and a practice that are inseparable.

From day to day, Payman, who had become an object for sale, saw other young Yazidi women—such as two of her cousins, Khalida and Nivya, who were considered more beautiful than she—being sold, whereas she was not. The men of ISIS even organized a beauty contest, thereby further humiliating and deepening the already immense pain of the young girls who didn't correspond to the aesthetic criteria of their torturers. Finally, she too found a buyer: a man from Tajikistan took her away from the prison and drove her, along with three other girls, to Manmij, in Syria. What she now relates is something I've never seen except in movies. But this is no movie. Often actual horror is as bad as or even worse than anything you could make up. I feel like screaming. All day long, she would remain locked up in some administrative building with other Yazidi women. Every night, the owners would come to collect their slaves and lock them up in "bedrooms."

In hers, Payman was attached to the bed with handcuffs, "like the ones the police have." On her wrists and ankles, the metal shackles were so tight that they left black and blue marks. And every night it was the same. I know pretty much what she's about to say. I've interviewed many Roma women who were raped in Macedonia and Romania. Automatically, I steel myself; it's only later, upon leaving the trailer, that I'm overcome with intense repulsion, a nausea that almost makes me vomit, in total disgust with mankind.

Two of Payman's sisters were also brought to this hellish place. She knows by heart the nationalities of the jailers: two Tajiks, two Chechens, one Iranian, and a Bosnian. Carefully, trying not to inflict even more pain, Sebar asks how the men of ISIS thought of the young women.

"Did they say you were their wives, that you would never be able to leave them?" I understand that she's trying to see how this account squares with Avine's. Payman shakes her head. As time went on the insults got worse: they called the Yazidi women their *sabyas*.

By all evidence, Payman's fate was even worse than Avine's—because she was not pretty enough. Four months went by that way. Sleepless nights, days spent trying to doze between interruptions by the man responsible for verifying that they were faithfully saying their prayers.

From what Payman said, the building in which she was imprisoned had five stories and a large number of rooms. In the daytime, the Yazidi women were tied to the bars on the windows, largely separated from each other. ISIS men came and went, as if this were the most normal thing in the world. No one spoke to them. A female slave of the Islamic State could be chained up anywhere, like a dog. Nobody seemed to see them. I can tell that Valy is particularly tense. As a Rom from Romania, he comes from the last enslaved people of Europe.

I thought I'd heard the worst, but Sebar suddenly asks a question that I've long been wondering about: "Did some women get pregnant?" I'm concentrating. ISIS's policy regarding Yazidi babies born in captivity concerns me: rape being both a weapon of war and a way to "compensate" fighters, it is statistically impossible that no babies were born of these systematic acts of aggression.

Payman confirms this. Where she was imprisoned, two women got pregnant. One was thirty years old and is now here in the Kadia camp. The other was sixteen, and she's still there. Their owners allowed them to carry their pregnancies to term. For the births, they were taken to a separate room, and a midwife came from the central hospital to assist. Immediately at birth, the two babies, girls, were torn from their mothers by an ISIS member. Given the usual total lack of human kindness, the use of a midwife to help the young slaves surprises me. I'd like to see in it a hint of compassion, but deep inside I know the true reason is something else entirely. Indeed, these babies aren't considered by the guards to be future slaves but rather potential Islamists. They're therefore precious and must be born perfectly healthy. Raised alongside the children of ISIS members, they're destined to become soldiers if they're boys, and if they are girls, they will be wives who will, in turn, give birth to soldiers. The midwife is there to ensure that the newborn is in good health. The young Yazidi women are nothing more than reproductive machines, to be eliminated if they don't give total satisfaction. Indeed, the two rapists were furious that the babies were girls: "We are going to get you pregnant again. We want boys. We want fighters. Otherwise, we'll kill you. Your daughter will be raised by us, and we will marry her off."

Sebar is surprised that Payman didn't become pregnant. In her sad, rough voice, the young Yazidi explains that her owner gave her pills "so that she wouldn't have a baby," for he was already married in Tajikistan, with three children; his wife, who had remained in the country, didn't know that he had gotten himself a slave. Four months later he died in combat, leaving Payman to the fate specified in his will. She was transferred to another Tajik who, after raping her, quickly sold her to a thirty-year-old Jordanian. The new owner locked her in an empty house. When he felt like it, he would force her to put on extravagant makeup and call her his *sabya*. A month and a half later, he sold her to an Algerian, who kept her for two months and sold her to another Tajik. In Raqqa, where he took her, she became the slave of his entire family, living with his wife and his three children.

For a long time, she was no longer called Payman. At the insistence of her owners, she was forced to change her name. The Tajik, whose wife treated her badly, sold her to an Iraqi.

I'm surprised Payman was sold and resold so many times. She comments bitterly that her masters systematically resold her because they were unsatisfied with her for some reason she didn't know. The Iraqi, who also owned two other Yazidi girls, Linda and Syban, from the same village as Payman, wanted to have children. Fortunately for Payman, Linda and Syban had birth control pills that she was able to take in secret.

Payman stayed with the Iraqi for two-and-a-half months before managing to escape. In the daytime, she was guarded by a man whose arm had been injured in a bombardment. He took pain relievers and often fell asleep. With a neighbor's help, Syban had been able to obtain a telephone, and she used it to call her family, who gave her the number of a smuggler. The girls gave him the address, and at nightfall they stole the guard's keys before piling into the car that was there waiting for them.

Since this meeting with Payman, I've interviewed a number of other young girls that the ISIS men didn't find attractive. Their fate, unfortunately, was often the same. Some were sold and resold more than ten times, carried off to towns and villages, locked up in office buildings or trailer camps near the oil wells in Iraq and Syria. The account by Payman, the stone-faced girl with dark eyes, reveals the true nature of the Islamists of ISIS, hidden beneath the patina of religion and costumed in the purity of the so-called caliphate.

The Yazidi women given to fighters or sold to the employees of the Islamic State are a foretaste of the paradise that the organization promises its members: impunity and omnipotence, riches, debauchery. The bound bodies of the Yazidi women reward jihadists with the carnal pleasures granted to martyrs in the afterlife, but which, in fact, they can experience on Earth, thanks to these female slaves. The bellies of these captives bring them sons and daughters, ensuring they will increase and prosper. Moreover, the women who are too old, the "useless" ones, are often gotten rid of. Their suffering stretches the boundaries of inhumanity.

Often, considering these young men, some of whom come from our European cities, I've wondered where the fearsomely potent Islamist ideology draws such strength that it fascinates them to the point where they're willing to abandon their homes, and our homelands, for hostile territory where death awaits. Today, I feel I understand to a certain degree: this ideology, for which they declare themselves ready to die, comes with total power, a kind of limitless sadistic pleasure. These young men leave because jihad offers them precisely the things that are lacking in their everyday lives: the feeling of invincibility and importance derived from fighting for a cause, the bearing of arms and permission to kill; wealth, stolen from the *kuffar*; and women, lots of women, submitting to their every desire.

The power of life and death, money, and sex: this is the formula for genocide. For this they are ready to die. Better to live a life of thrills for a few months than spend dozens of years in a life in Europe that seems banal to them. The supposed superman, armed with absolute truth, has no fear of death.

THE TAILOR OF RAQQA

August 10, 2015–Essian camp

Fatigue is making itself felt. I'm less and less able to withstand the 124-degree heat of summer in Iraq. The sun has become a pitiless enemy that nothing can escape. My head is spinning. The rest of the team is struggling too. Even the rare spots of shade don't really help. Souhaib, our red-haired go-between, leads the way among the white canvas tents. Space is limited, the atmosphere stifling. Here and there, carefree children play in the sand, seemingly unaware of the tragedy that surrounds them.

Souhaib points out one of the makeshift dwellings. Bahar is standing there, apparently waiting for us. Round-cheeked and shy, she bears the scars of her recent captivity. She still looks extremely disturbed and will remain that way for a long time but nevertheless wishes to speak, however painful it may be. She keeps repeating that she wants the world to know what she has been through, what they've all endured.

One of her older brothers, standing before the tent, is agitated and furious and attempts to intervene. He's shouting and making threats, fearful that we're journalists and tomorrow his sister's face will be in the international press. He's terrified at the thought that the affront already inflicted might become public knowledge and his family's pain and shame will make headlines—fueling compassion, shock, and discussion maybe, but making it impossible for them to put the horror they've experienced behind them.

Often families are reluctant to allow the victims, especially women, to speak. Yazidi society remains a traditional one: a woman who has been raped is a woman soiled, ruined, lost. The horror of the tortures is compounded by the disgrace, with which she'll have to learn to live as best she can. The women who've been tortured suffer double punishment: their return home is tainted by the fear of how they'll be viewed. One of them tells me, after hours of discussion, "Before, nobody had touched me. From now on, even if I'm with my family, nothing will ever be the same."

These young women must keep quiet, keep their abuse secret, and go on with their lives without describing or detailing the horrors that others can only imagine. For the sake of decency, they must pretend to forget as quickly as possible, going through the motions of their lives "before," although everything has changed.

Zaher negotiates in a soft voice with the older brother for a long while. Little by little, the voices grow quiet, the flow of words slows. And then there's silence. Zaher approaches, gesturing with his hand: "It's OK; he says yes."

Bahar is sitting silently in front of a pile of colorful blankets and small mattresses that are the sole furnishings of this family of refugees, which have been set aside to make room before nightfall, when they'll all pile back into the tent to sleep.

Bahar is from Ayn Fathi, a village I'm not familiar with, which, with Valy's help, we've been trying for a long time to locate on the map. She's eighteen years old. Like Payman, she looks much older, marked by the gravity of her ordeal. Eighteen. At home, that's the age when young people are intoxicated with the freedom of newly acquired adulthood and rites of passage like graduating from high school, getting a driver's license, and starting college—a future opening before them, still carefree. Here, for Bahar, it signifies the end of a year of slavery, rapes, and confronting absolute violence.

As usual, we've brought the heavy orange folder of photographs. Without even waiting for us to explain the procedure, Bahar starts leafing through it. Her eyes wander distractedly from one picture to the next. Suddenly, she regains focus. Her eyes light up. "I know him!" Intrigued, I glance at the photograph.

The photo doesn't look as if it was taken by a professional. It shows a tailor in his workshop: in the background on the left is a pile of uniforms wrapped in clear plastic; on the right, hanging on a metal wire, some "Afghan" outfits; in the foreground a small off-white sewing machine. "The tailor's shop was right next to the place where I was held."

Nothing very special at first glance, except it seems to me that Bahar isn't the first to stop at that picture. I question Valy, who confirms it: a few days earlier Avine, seeing the workshop made of sheet metal, had the same reaction—"The tailor in Raqqa." I can't believe it; I'm more used to showing pictures from the German archives to villagers from Russia and Belarus, often eighty years old, so few of whom remember—they would shrug their shoulders dubiously: "I don't recognize anyone."

There are several snapshots of the tailor, who seems rather pleased to be so popular. He poses with customers who've come to order or pick up a piece of clothing. These photos, so banal in appearance, spur my curiosity. I have a feeling they're more significant than they seem at first glance, but I can't quite put my finger on their hidden meaning. Up till now, I've been paying more attention to the many shots of the horrors perpetrated by the Islamic State that are so prevalent on our social media. In order to understand these crimes and to imprint them in my memory, I've been trying to penetrate the murderous logic at work. The tailor's workshop, so banal and similar to so many others I've come across, particularly in the Middle East where often it's the men who practice this trade, hadn't drawn my attention.

But I recall now the conversation we had about the tailor. Avine had gone to his shop to order clothes not only for Abu J., her owner, but also for her nephews who had been kidnapped by ISIS.

Bahar lived near the tailor's studio shown in the photo. She had therefore been able to observe the comings and goings of the customers. "The foreigners who came to Raqqa had their uniforms made there. I saw Frenchmen and Australians. They used to place their orders and come back a few days later." She leans forward to examine the scene captured on glossy paper, and goes on, "Look, that one, that customer is Abu W. He's Egyptian. He used to come and pick up his clothes. I remember."

In a flash, I finally understand. The tailor in Raqqa, self-proclaimed capital of the Islamic State, is not just any tradesman. His shop is a mandatory stop for the men of ISIS as well as certain female slaves. Dressing in ISIS style is a rite of entry: for the new recruits, donning the uniform is the sign of integration into the "State," allegiance and acceptance of its values. For the slaves, it's a cloth prison intended to banish their freedom and their Yazidi identity. For the "free" men and women, as well as for the captives, the uniform symbolizes belonging to the Islamic State. The wearer becomes part of the whole: it is an act that is by definition the point of no return, whether accomplished by free will or by force. To dress in ISIS style is to become part of the Islamic State.

In a dictatorship, whatever its ideological underpinnings, the uniformity of clothing contributes to the dissolution of individual identity into a larger dominant entity that is supposedly the bearer of truth. And any truth that claims to be absolute risks becoming dangerous—often murderous, as exemplified in Europe by the Nazis. Seventy years after the war ended, the old *kolkhoz* members of the former Soviet Union still recall without any hesitation the color of the uniforms of those who came to their collective farm to gun down Jews. The venomous ideology of the Nazi murderers was garbed in its own color: often black, sometimes green.

Entering the workshop of the tailor from Raqqa is a symbolic step of integration into the Islamic State, and it is for that reason that certain "customers" insisted on immortalizing the scene: their visible initiation into the caliphate. The donning of a uniform that is at once military, religious, and terrorist.

At nightfall, when we take our leave of Bahar, I feel a curious mixture of contradictory emotions, as if the young woman had transmitted her state of mind to me: troubled, disturbed, and traumatized, wanting to strike her horrible experience from my mind but invested with the responsibility to bear witness, to prevent the ISIS criminals from going unpunished, a vow she made in Raqqa. In spite of the aftereffects and the still-fresh wounds whose scars would perhaps never disappear, Bahar wants to testify before the witness stand of history, to describe the cogs of the terrorist war machine that only those who have lived within it can reveal.

The tailor from Raqqa is one of those cogs. Moreover, other Yazidi survivors would later identify him, demonstrating the significance of this unimportant little man. He's not simply a tradesman running a small business in the streets of the capital of the Islamic State; he's one of the entry points into the murderous society of ISIS, a link in the totalitarian machine. The terrifying genocidal machine—oh, so human.

In the streets of Raqqa, the tailor isn't the only one to trade on his craft. Other professions serve the ends of ISIS; other workers offer their skills to the jihadists: some forced to do it, some out of opportunism. It's always a better deal to do business with the authorities than to resist them. These menial jobs contribute in their own way to the smooth functioning of the Islamic State, each adding its stone to the edifice. To be sure, sewing a uniform is no big thing. But just as there is no such thing as a small act of resistance, there is no such thing as a small contribution to a crime.

Doctors play an important role too. In Raqqa, the hospital is open for business. The medical corps provides health services to the men of ISIS, not only caring for the injured and the sick but also participating in the torture of the Yazidis. Medicine, put to evil use, is omnipresent: verifying the virginity of the girls, administering drugs, delivering babies of women who have become pregnant through rape. Bahar told us that at the prison in Badush, near Mosul, where she was locked up, the water and food given to prisoners were adulterated: the jailers would add a syrup that made the captives dizzy and sometimes knocked them out. The drug was supposed to keep them from complaining by making them forget that they would surely never see their loved ones again.

Another woman who was held captive in Mosul relates the same thing: "They would put something into the food. We were often exhausted; we slept all day long. That's why we were unable to escape. Today, I'm still tired. I have trouble carrying my child, and I often have a fever."

These chemical straitjackets, like the anesthesia used in raping the young slaves or the pills used on the children, can't be administered without some type of medical supervision. You have to know what to give, how much, and for what purpose.

FILMING ISIS

August 11, 2015—Dilshad Palace

The coffee is as bitter as ever. Breakfast is spare, consisting essentially of dried fruits. It's not as early as usual. We've decided to remain at the hotel today, to organize our material and rest a little before leaving in the evening. There's no sense in rushing when you're investigating genocide.

Yesterday, we got back late from the Essian camp, exhausted by the hours spent listening to the memories of the horrors suffered, haunted by the image of Bahar and the reverberations of her testimony. Despite that, within the shelter of my room at the end of the long beige corridor, I was unable to sleep—not for the first time. Since the beginning of this trip, my nights have been a reflection of the lives encountered in this country—amputated. How could I feel at ease in this hotel, knowing that just a few kilometers from my comfortable room, all these people, whom I've known long enough to appreciate, whose faces are forever etched in my heart, are sleeping in a refugee camp, their only hope for the future being some hypothetical exile in Europe?

Since our arrival, we have collected and recorded a large amount of testimony. It's time to step back and listen again, analyze, cross-check, and dig deeper into certain points. So we take out our road maps, spread them out on the table, and talk, exchanging points of view and impressions. As we progress, links form among the stories: connections that suddenly shed light on some aspects that up to now were unclear.

When you listen to many victims over a short period of time, your brain ends up retaining only certain ones. It's beyond your control. All the words remain, but they get jumbled, and it becomes difficult to be sure which of the people we questioned said them. A small number of witnesses therefore become emblematic, the embodiment of a common testimony. Such is the case of the people described in this book.

While we're listening once again to Avine's testimony, one name jumps out: Al-Naïm Square. The young girl mentions having gone there several times during her captivity, dressed as an ISIS woman, and later, during her escape. "The smuggler's wife, my cousin, and I went to the market during Ramadan. Next to the statue in Al-Naïm Square, they killed a woman by shooting her twelve times. She was naked. They executed her because she had killed her husband, who was an ISIS soldier."

At the time, we hadn't paid much attention to this story, one account of a murder among others. Avine had witnessed so many. But something attracts my attention, and I'm not the only one. Zaher and Valy furrow their brows too. Like me, they remember that yesterday Bahar also spoke a lot about Al-Naïm Square.

I turn on my computer and open Google Maps. In the search bar, I type "Al-Naïm Square, Raqqa." Oddly enough, I come upon a bar or pastry shop, perhaps a restaurant—it's hard to tell exactly—that has the name Café Al-Naïm.

I'm about to close the page when I notice that twenty-five subscribers have recently posted comments about the café. The internet never ceases to amaze me. Social networks have connected to the least city, the most modest little restaurant to the entire planet, even though it happens to be located in the capital of the Islamic State. I scroll through the comments, which are for the most part virulent: "If you come, you will be killed!" "The bearded ones are everywhere!" "If you phone, they'll cut your hand off!" Another customer mentions that he met his seventh wife there.

I can't get over the fact that I'm able to read the opinions of customers of a bar located in the heart of the territory conquered by ISIS. I can't help thinking, *If the internet had existed in 1942, what kind of comments would have been posted by the customers of a bar located near Auschwitz?* The internet has united the world; that can't be denied. Still, it seems to me that we try not to think too much about it, to persuade ourselves that there are absolute limits, differences between dictatorships and democracies, between places where unthinkable atrocities are committed and our peaceful streets. We like to pretend that mass crimes are far away, cut off from our universe, that they happen in some other isolated place. Our desire to sleep peacefully has no limits. It shuts us up in hermetic imaginary bubbles that deform our reality to make it carefree. Insouciance is the little sister of irresponsibility. With the internet, it's possible to reserve a table in a restaurant in Raqqa, one of the crime capitals of our time, after checking to see that the food is good. With the internet, hell is within keyboard range, but if one agrees to see it, the question arises: you who are aware, what have you done to help your brother?

In 1942, it was possible not to know. That is no longer the case today. The computer we all have is a window on the whole world. ISIS understands this very well.

On the recording of Bahar's testimony, I search for the passage about Al-Naïm Square. When she mentions it, the weariness shows on her face. We've been speaking for several hours already. One of the photos in the orange binder gets her talking: she recognizes the statue in the square. "The ISIS men, this is where they decapitate people." I push her to go on and ask her if she has witnessed that type of execution with her own eyes. "I was present," she answers without flinching.

On two occasions her owner, Tara, an Australian woman who bought her as a gift for her husband, took her to watch beheadings. In total, she saw fifteen people die that way. The condemned were men as well as women, all dressed in orange. The executioners were impossible to identify: dressed entirely in black, with only their eyes visible. They cut off the heads with a precise stroke of a large sword, or else they sprayed the bodies with bullets.

The executions seemed to Bahar to take a long time. Five hours, she said. That length of time surprises me, especially since there wasn't a large number of victims. I finally understand what she neglects to mention, no doubt because it seems obvious to her: these beheadings were filmed. It is the setting up, the staging of the executions that explains their length and the apparent calm of the victims. When the scene didn't look right, the "actors" repeated it, so much so that the victims, who screamed at the beginning, ended up silent. The speech pronounced by the executioners before the fatal blow had to be clearly audible. The "director," according to her account, an ISIS sheikh, sat apart from the others, coordinating the camera work without allowing himself to be filmed. Nevertheless, he spoke, and his voice could be heard. In that way, the person who ordered the executions and those who carried them out remained faceless. They could be anyone at all; they could be everywhere.

Bahar goes on talking: "The ISIS men placed us. We had to remain standing. The Australian woman's children got very excited and chanted, 'Allah Akbar!' and 'The Islamic State will endure!'" Bahar had to shout along with them, show her joy, her exaltation, so she wouldn't be suspected of being a traitor. The rest of the spectators, and there were many of them, chanted together. Afterwards, the ISIS men filmed the severed heads, holding them up by the hair. She adds, "They smeared the bodies with a white powder that looked like sugar and made them melt."

Bahar is very disturbed by the memory of these moments, as we can see from her posture. She's testifying as a victim who has been forced to cross the red line, someone who was unable to refuse.

I stop the recording. I reflect: Avine, Bahar. These young girls, present in Al-Naïm Square or any other execution site—what becomes of them when they're unable to escape? Everybody has a breaking point. Forcibly converted, their names changed, subjected to violence, dressed in religious garb that isn't their own, living in the midst of a group that is united and sure of its convictions, to which they are forced to pretend adherence—did their will break, did it get worn away?

Today, Avine and Bahar have become Yazidis once more. They're courageous and determined. But who were they, under their *niqabs*, when they pretended to scream with joy while cheering on beheadings? I would like to think that every hour of every day of their captivity they remained Yazidis and resisted being converted. But I know that human self-awareness is complicated, tangled, and at times impossible to understand. I can't help imagining that in order to survive the beatings, the threats, the fear, they perhaps ended up thinking, speaking, and acting like ISIS members.

I'm not judging—quite the opposite—but I am agreeing to hear the pain of these victims, their weaknesses, without burdening them with the guilt of not being heroes.

Al-Naïm Square in Raqqa is thus one of the recurring film locations for the Islamic State. Further research on the web confirms this. With a few clicks, I come upon a scene of crucifixion. The square looks big. On the crosses, which are attached to metal grills, are tied the bodies of two men. They are dead. Facing them is a small group of passersby, one of whom is holding a bicycle. Another, a young man, is wearing a yellow tee-shirt and beige slacks. They are deciphering something written on the large paper sign that is glued to the cadavers. Others, farther away, pay no attention to them. Later on, I'll meet a young Yazidi boy who saw numerous decapitated bodies in the course of his detention. The "justification" for their execution was written on signs in Arabic. According to him, in certain parts of Raqqa large screens had been installed so that the executions could be viewed from far away.

The population of Raqqa has gotten used to living next to and attending these executions, which are frequent, just as we get used to the horrifying videos brought to us by the internet. ISIS propaganda, both in its territory and beyond its borders, is frighteningly effective, well thought-out, and organized. One look at the videos makes this clear. There is a catchy little tune, sung in Arabic; a convoy of vehicles sporting black flags that snap in the wind; prisoners in orange jumpsuits whose heads are cut off by bearded, pitiless executioners to musical accompaniment. The videos of the Islamic State go viral. They're hard to avoid; even the major Western information channels broadcast portions of them, especially when the victim is a Westerner. The soldiers of the Islamic State preserve everything for posterity—attacks, training, murders, and so on—and the images of their abuses, which are at once instruments of terror and tools of propaganda, inundate the internet.

The Yazidis are unwilling actors in, but also witnesses of, the Islamic State's films, as with Bahar and the beheadings in Al-Naïm Square or the murder of a Jordanian pilot who was burned alive. Muath Al-Kasasbeh was captured on December 24, 2014, in Syria after his plane had crashed into a lake while he was striking ISIS positions. His murder was announced on February 3, 2015. I wanted to watch the video in the hope of gaining some understanding. It shows the Jordanian pilot dressed in orange walking before a row of men in military garb, who are armed to the teeth as he calmly enters his cage. Then an ISIS soldier lights a torch and ignites a line of gasoline that runs up to the jail. The rest is hard to watch. The pilot dies on his knees.

Later on, we meet another witness, a young Yazidi boy who knows the story of the pilot's murder well. His name is Amin. The interview takes place in a little unfinished house in the region of Dohuk. He's twelve years old. He had been bought in Iraq along with his mother, then brought to Raqqa. He was there the day of the arrest of Muath Al-Kasasbeh, who had had to eject from his burning plane. His capture was photographed, too, and the images spread through the social networks. They show him, without his uniform, surrounded by several ISIS men who, with a particularly twisted flourish, have thrown their arms over his shoulders in an almost comradely way.

During the interview, Amin looks at the photos. They show the pilot accompanied by the group that has captured him. He reacts: "That is not the way it happened." He points at the man in the middle. "He's the one who caught the pilot, him alone. They took the picture afterwards. All those people only got there afterwards so they could be in the photo." So, lots of ISIS men had been eager to be in the souvenir snapshot and had come running in order to pose.

I'm familiar with this phenomenon. How many young German members of the Wehrmacht had rushed over to be photographed at the sites of the shootings of Jews by the *Einsatzgruppen*? The murder of others, on a day of genocide, isn't only an attraction in itself; it also spurs a desire to immortalize oneself, alive alongside those who kill and those who die.

Avine had been taken by Abu J. to the murder and cremation of the pilot. She stood next to him, to the left of the cameraman. When we question her, she gives us specific details about the "conditions" under which the filming took place. She explains that the "framer" had them rehearse the Jordanian pilot entering the iron cage to ensure an optimal shot. She also tells us what the framer hadn't wanted to show: there were people around the cage, many people, who aren't visible in the images published on the internet. The cameraman asked them not to move or talk, and not to shout, "Allah Akbar," so that the filming would not be disrupted.

These two witnesses to the death of the Jordanian pilot opened my eyes not only to the staging of ISIS's murders but also to the local interest they aroused. The "neighbors" like to attend public death sentences.

The propaganda vehicles used by ISIS are many and varied, from simple videos filmed on cell phones and transmitted via Facebook to quasi-professional films, rehearsed, acted, and produced. This is a multifaceted, well-oiled industry that takes advantage of the flexibility of today's social networks. The Islamic State has successfully managed to inscribe barbarity into the modern multimedia landscape.

The videos of the murders of Yazidis seem to be more restrained than the macabre staging of the murders of foreigners. ISIS publicity ranges from amateur films—aimed above all at insiders, idiosyncratic little productions designed to show off their exploits to the community, to make a name and a place for the makers—to major productions, snuff movies so polished that they look like they came straight out of Hollywood studios.

I'm reminded of Lawin's testimony about the shooting deaths of the men of Kojo captured on a cell phone, which brings to mind the German cameramen in the pretty little Austro-Hungarian city of Lvov, which was part of Ukraine in September 1941. Perched on top of a military truck opposite the Briguitta prison, they were there to film, from above, the pogrom they had orchestrated. With fists and sticks, the Ukrainians isolated the Jews. The older women were stripped and thrown to the ground. I'm unable to forget the terrible image of one of them, heavy-set, who was running, almost naked, wearing one shoe, with a Ukrainian boy carrying a cudgel following close on her heels.

In 2004, I returned to the scene of the crime and the filming. Nothing had changed. Only one tree, an involuntary witness to genocide, had thickened a bit. Today, the German photos are exhibited on the walls of Holocaust museums in Jerusalem and Washington. I refuse to allow photos of the massacre of the Yazidis to decorate the rooms of a museum someday. Genocides should not engender museums. They should mobilize the international community to do everything to put a stop to them.

I'm at once fascinated and frightened by the human race's ability to go on with its history while a part of itself is being annihilated. The murderous, predatory, archaic practice of massacres seems in no way to obstruct the smooth functioning of institutions, the administration of societies, and the thought processes of those who govern them. Many thinkers prefer not to think about this. The values of modern democracies accommodate themselves to mass murders when they have their roots outside the territory they administer. People today cannot avoid being aware of mass crimes. Nevertheless, just like their predecessors, they tolerate blood being shed so long as its stains fall somewhere else.

LEAVING

July 29–August 11, 2015

Two weeks have gone by. We have listened to dozens of broken lives, hundreds of blood-soaked stories, thousands of painful words. It's time to get back on an airplane and smile at the flight attendant—perhaps the same one as when we came, but he'll certainly have no memory of us, because he'll have seen so many faces pass by. Plus we've changed too. Our skin is parched from the sun and stressed by our fatigue, the weight of the atrocities we've heard, and the responsibility we now bear.

We're going home, but the mission is far from done. We must translate, compile, transcribe, analyze. The task is hard. Hours and hours of recordings, nonstop atrocities.

The silhouettes of the Yazidis of Essian, Kadia, and the other camps populate my nightmares. I write, anxious to give physical form to the cries of the victims. So many things to say, so many words to invest with meaning. Still, I know from experience that understanding the workings of genocide takes time. It means listening to large numbers of victims in order to match their testimonies, to identify their corroborating elements.

December 16, 2015—Paris

I am walking through the Place de la République. In my haste, I slip on the paving stones. The atmosphere of Paris, especially here, is heavy, soulless, emptied of its legendary lightness. Paris is no longer a feast. A month and three days after the terrorist attacks. One hundred thirty dead, murdered; three hundred and fifty injured. Sitting on a terrace, standing in a concert hall, young people were killed by other young people claiming allegiance to the Islamic State after having been trained in Syria, for the most part. The unthinkable has hit home. The foul beast has killed in our streets.

Flickering candles and sad bouquets are strewn around the monument of the Republic. Passersby pay their respects to the photos of the victims. Their silence in the middle of Paris impresses me. The front has moved; the war declared by ISIS is being exported. It's no longer some faraway confrontation. It's no longer only about the people of the Middle East. It has become our problem. The victims are some of our own. In reality, it has always been that way, but today it is no longer possible to close our eyes. That is my hope, at least.

I walk up Magenta Boulevard. Parisians are avoiding looking at each other for fear, perhaps, of showing how upset they are and how helpless they feel but probably also out of fear of others at a time when everyone is being warned to resist the enemy. I buy *Le Monde* at a kiosk. Every day the paper publishes articles on several of the 130 victims, giving each one a face. I'm proud of my country, which, in its way, is paying homage to each life cut down by these criminals.

Thousands are being murdered far away by the same people who are shooting right here, among us. In Iraq, in Syria, those who have been massacred remain nameless: Yazidis, Christians, Muslims. In those lands, so familiar and yet so unknown to the West, they are nothing more than statistics. The faces and the names of the killers are sometimes reported by the international press; the victims are usually—although not always—merely counted. A massacre, a suicide killer who blows himself up, a bombing becomes, for a day, a faceless statistic: "Twenty-three dead in a bomb attack in Baghdad," we read. In France up to now, we've refused to simply count. The memorial in *Le Monde*, with its photos, its words, keeps us from collaborating in the bookkeeping logic of the killers.

I close the door to the offices, which are installed in a large classic Paris apartment. At my computer, I try to finish a chapter I started several days ago. I am unable to do it. I think of the terrorists who assaulted Paris with their well-rehearsed methods, learned in Syria or Iraq or even in France, the same methods being taught to Yazidi children.

Everywhere, on all the TV stations, the radio, in the newspapers, specialists of all stripes—pundits, geopoliticians, sociologists, philosophers, experts in all conceivable genres—are squaring off, issuing analyses. For a while, the French people are hungry for explanations. Sometimes I catch myself thinking that these opinions are being broadcast to the saturation point, in an attempt to understand, of course, but also to avoid thinking more. Mass murder, thoroughly dissected, can be filed away in the category of what we know and can forget. For us, the Cartesian French, thinking is a way of reassuring ourselves: I think, therefore I am living.

A part of the answer is over there, under the sun of Iraq, in the hearts and memories of Yazidi survivors. The first trip allowed us to discover some small pieces of it. The need for a return visit has become self-evident. People often ask me why my team and I go to Iraq. I always answer: because they're killing people. Because the genocide of the Yazidis is going on right now.

Time to go back.

THE BROTHELS OF MOSUL

February 13, 2016—Kadia camp
Trailer D17

It was in Guatemala, in 2013, I believe, in the lovely green mountains of the Quiché region. The sloping road snaked through summits covered with lush vegetation. The shade of large trees sheltered the coffee bushes. We had come to this place, far from the noisy, hectic capital, to interview survivors of the armed conflict that had ravaged the country for more than two decades. Seventeen years after the end of the conflict (the peace accords were signed in 1996), the memory of the many civilian victims was alive and painful.

Andrej Umanski had prepared the records and made the trip with us. For over ten years, he has been working alongside us looking for mass graves. In the car taking us to the scene of the tragedy, his eyes fixed on the records, he kept repeating, dumbfounded: "Not far from here, there is a village where several hundred inhabitants were killed." Our translator, Margarita, with her bright eyes and jet-black hair, speaks Quiché and Spanish and is a native of the area. She was worried: "It's dangerous to go to an isolated area. Also, there are gold mines near here. It's really risky." I insisted, of course.

The village was calm, silent. Some Quiché women, sitting in the shade in front of humble dwellings, were weaving bands of traditional cloth. They all pointed out the house of the Mayan priest a little farther on—a survivor, they said, of shootings orchestrated by the military. But we had to wait while he said his prayers—Mayan prayers.

Curious, I nevertheless approached his house and went in through a very low door. He was sitting on a little stool looking at some black beans that he had just thrown on a table. He seemed to be concentrating, indifferent to our intrusion. There were three of us, pressed up against each other, waiting for the ritual to end. He again tossed the beans, then, looking at us, predicted a great future for Yahad. I remained silent. Then, inviting us to go outside in the fresh air, he and his wife gave testimony facing the camera, seated around a large table. While they were talking, I couldn't take my eyes off a dog, lying under the white wooden table around which we were seated, on which the priest's wife was resting her feet, a living cushion.

The priest had been part of a local patrol under the orders of the military, charged with tracking communist supporters of guerrilla forces that were hidden in the mountains. In spite of their intensive efforts, they found nothing. One day when the priest returned from the forest empty-handed, he was horrified to find his entire family massacred, motionless around the breakfast table, each person killed by a bullet to the head. Women and children. In every dwelling, the same desolate scene.

In our eyes, his story instantly transformed the attractively decorated houses surrounding us into so many scenes of murder. The soldiers who had committed these crimes herded the men of the patrol into the center of the village and said: "Now that your families are dead, are you going to work for us?" In unison, the fathers of the decimated families replied in the negative. The soldiers then shot half of them. The remaining twenty gave in. In order to survive.

A former military man accompanying us whispered to me: "That was our strategy. They didn't want to do the dirty work, so the whole village was wiped out, until the last ones who were left worked with us. Strategy!"

That encounter profoundly changed my way of listening and my understanding of mass murders. For the first time, I met a man who had lost everything and, in order to survive, had had no other choice than to become, in turn, an armed accomplice of the criminals who had massacred his loved ones. It was troubling; I couldn't picture it; it seemed impossible, inconceivable. This absolute victim, this man who had suffered in his body and his soul, had been seared with a red-hot iron, deprived of the thing that meant the most to him and transformed into a participant in the very crime that had victimized his family. For a long time, I put this unsettling encounter aside. If reality had forced me to say 1=2, I could not have been more disturbed. I preferred to continue thinking that 1=1 and 2=2, even though the reality of mass crime had challenged my certainty.

I hadn't anticipated meeting the same twisting of humanity here in Iraqi Kurdistan. ISIS, like the military brigades in Guatemala, crushes certain of its victims to turn them into not only subjugated slaves but also collaborators—or auxiliaries, rather, even apprentice jihadists. All the witnesses we met were broken to some degree or another.

Sharmin is no exception to the rule.

It all started with a phone call while we were still in Brussels, deep in preparation for the second trip: "A young Yazidi woman has just been freed after a long period of imprisonment, more than a year."

We're back in Iraq a few weeks later, and we're getting ready to meet her. We are preparing to film a woman abused by ISIS—*yet another one,* we think. The words are terrible. On the way, I ask myself whether the length of time she had been held captive affected her relations with ISIS more than was the case for the other witnesses we've met so far. I share this with Valy. "In my opinion, that's the way we should orient the interview," he answers. Then we say no more. We shall see. . . .

We no longer look at the road that leads to the camps. We are preparing for what's coming next. I stare off into space. I know every little curve in the road, the potholes, and the lumps of dirt in the middle of the pavement. The road to the camps is from now on the path to our investigation.

Sharmin is attractively dressed, very dignified. Right from the start, I realize that she doesn't know how old she is. "I don't know, I am not sure," she says, hesitating. Then she takes a guess: around twenty. What kind of life can these young Yazidis in the villages near Mount Sinjar have had, to make her unsure of her age? Her eyes try to smile, but instead they fill with tears.

She's from Kojo. She recounts her arrest, a process we've heard described many times, but she insists on one particular point: there was a specific clan that came to arrest the towns-people of Kojo and steal their belongings, a clan from Tal Afar. Neighbors, just like with Lawin and the others. You cannot have genocide without neighbors.

Sharmin was bought by someone named Abu B. on August 15, 2014. That man, married to two of Sharmin's cousins, didn't take her to his house. He locked her in a room in the hotel in Mosul, as was the case for many other young women. The first night he tore off her clothes and raped her brutally. Then he brought in his four bodyguards and passed her on to them. Unfortunately, the nightmare was just beginning.

In all the time we've been conducting our research, this is the first time a young woman is describing openly, in front of the whole team, the sexual violence she has endured. Surprised, we look at each other in silence in order not to interrupt. Sharmin's confessions simply mean that she has nothing more to lose and she refuses to allow her pain, which is all she has left, to be kept secret.

Little by little, we realize that Sharmin wasn't simply a sex slave; her jailers didn't treat her like a *sabya*. She was a prostitute. Men paid her owner to come and rape her, locked in a brothel hotel of the caliphate. I heard persistent rumors about the Islamic State's houses of prostitution but have never gotten direct testimony about them. I am all ears.

"ISIS likes money," she says over and over. She's right. But how could prostitution and pimping be legal in the Islamic State, a territory ruled by Sharia? How can ISIS authorize men to get rich by selling the bodies of slaves, by trading rape for money? Are the pimps of Mosul guided by law or by desire for material gain?

Sharmin remembers that every afternoon, at around five o'clock, she was forced to drink a substance that put her to sleep. In the middle of the night, often after midnight, unknown men would parade in. Most of them were local people, Iraqis from Mosul, but there were also foreigners: Saudis, Germans. That surprises me. I interrupt and ask her to repeat, "Germans?" She says yes. They weren't young, between forty and fifty years old. I press her. "German immigrants?" No. "German Germans." I wonder silently, what on earth would Germans over forty years old be doing in Mosul? To this day, I haven't found the answer.

Valy suddenly feels ill. He leaves the trailer and shuts himself in his car, parked nearby. We all have our personal pain, our weak spots, cracks in our shells, which is why we need to work as a team to carry out our investigations. Not everyone can take everything. Sharmin readjusts her black scarf, wipes her eyes, then stares off into the distance, back there, perhaps, and goes on with her testimony.

Sold three times, each time in the city of Mosul; locked up three times; and prostituted in different hotels, tied up in dark rooms where men came, paid their money, and raped her, over and over and over. She doesn't remember how many men crossed the threshold of the room that had become her cell. There were too many to count.

This isn't the first time I've heard about forced prostitution in the context of genocide. Later, when I got back home, I found on my computer the deposition of a young German, a soldier in 1942, whom Sharmin's story reminded me of. His testimony remains etched in my memory. He was visiting a friend of his, an SS man stationed in Kertch, in Crimea, during the Second World War:

> One day when I was to deliver a tablecloth for Lieutenant Schiller, who was working with Hauptstrumführer Finger, I wasn't able to find Finger in the place where he was staying. I was in SS quarters, a former school or public building in Kertch. There was a long hallway lined with doors to each of the rooms. I went to the second floor and entered the first room. When I opened the door, I saw an SS man lying on the bed with a pretty young girl next to him. Since this SS man couldn't tell me where Finger was, I went into a second room. There I also found a young girl with an SS man. As he didn't give me any information either, I went into a third room. There, lying on the bed, was an SS man out of uniform, just wearing pants. Next to him, that is to say on the edge of the bed, was a very young and pretty girl. I saw her caress the chin of the SS man, and I heard her say, "Tell me, Franz, you're not going to shoot me!" The girl was very young and spoke fluent German without an accent.

In Kertch in 1942 under Nazi dictatorship, just as in Mosul in 2015 under the black flag of the Islamic State, the authorization to kill Jews and Roma, viewed as subraces in the one case, and Yazidis, viewed as *kuffar* in the other, is communicated at all levels, from top to bottom. It goes with authorization to rape women and steal the belongings of families. The order to kill, and to die in order to kill, seems always to be accompanied by permission to rape. Like the Nazis, ISIS has placed rape at the heart of its war machine.

The Islamic State has organized daily life with absolute lucidity. The morale of the troops must be maintained so that the soldiers will not desert. This implies, in particular, providing brothels, even if they obviously contradict the values that are supposedly being upheld. Sharmin explains that in Mosul there are many houses where this forced prostitution is practiced—over a hundred, according to her. On the ground floor is a restaurant reserved for ISIS men; upstairs, a brothel. In that way, the combatants don't have to move around. They can eat and rape in the same building.

I sigh. ISIS's radical Islam, like Nazism, in no way elevates the human spirit, contrary to its claims. ISIS is not creating *Ubermenschen*. The unlimited authorization of brutal sex and the lure of looted wealth are what seal the commitment. The killers who shot Jews and Roma wouldn't have withstood the hardships of the glacial Russian winters, much less the creeping certainty that they weren't going to win the war against the Bolsheviks, without the raping and pillaging. Those young men, some of them well educated, wouldn't have killed civilians every day for three years without the terrible reward of sex and financial gain. Iraqis, Syrians, foreigners from far away—the men of ISIS would certainly not endure a radical way of life under the punishing sun of the

THE BROTHELS OF MOSUL

Iraqi summers and the rain of winter without stolen sex, money, or jewels.

The human race is made of the same raw material everywhere, and the jihadists are part of it.

The distinction that ISIS makes between its men and the *kuffar* gives them permission to kill, steal, and rape. It in no way signifies a higher degree of humanity. The only reason they believe themselves to be superior is that they grant themselves the right to kill other men, whom they view as inferior and cursed, even if they claim otherwise. They are nothing but mass criminals of the modern world. Being authorized to kill in the name of what they believe to be God doesn't make them moral, even from the perspective of their own beliefs, as attested by the numerous houses of prostitution lining the streets of Mosul. Without them, without a reward, maintaining a stable fighting force in the name of ideology alone would be much more of a utopian, even illusory, fantasy.

Foreign combatants from Europe or elsewhere are attracted by tangible promises, added to the ideal that offers them a position of superiority in the human race, a place where they can become rich and give free rein to their basest urges. There is no such thing as a purely religiously motivated crime, because the criminals cannot free themselves of sadism, rape, and theft. The clay that humanity is made of is impervious to the toughest ideologies.

The videos of the Islamic State's crimes are invading our screens. But the sexual violence and the looting of goods remain for the most part hidden from the public. If the men of ISIS are so proud of the rapes and the "legal" humiliations of Yazidi girls and women, why don't they commit them in front of the cameras? Decapitation and crucifixion ordered by an Islamic judge are awarded places of honor, so why don't they show those young women locked up in basements, tied to their beds of pain? Why don't they show off the black canvas bags filled with telephones, jewelry, and money they load into their cars when they arrest Yazidis if those abuses are also for the glory of the religious ideology they claim to uphold and defend? The murder of "inferiors" is proudly flaunted; rape and pillage are camouflaged.

They slit throats in public and exhibit their trophies, just as *Einsatzgruppen* shooters paraded before the cameras for propaganda purposes. But they rape and steal in secret, just like the young Germans of the SS in the shadow of the Gestapo, like criminals aware that their crimes toward women, once shown, will tarnish their grandeur.

The Islam of ISIS doesn't elevate the human being away from his criminal condition, his vilest urges. Worse, it justifies them. The crimes that are filmed, staged like the massive public execution in Palmyra, are to the Islamic State what the parades in Nuremberg were to the Nazis: a vain attempt to put themselves above the human race, with the right to kill or let live. The superman exists, in images at least, while the filming goes on. But the context has changed. In 1942, they were goose-stepping before the Führer and raping Jewish girls in the Soviet countryside; in 2016, they are cutting off heads with a knife, proudly shooting while professing submission to the caliphate and paying a procurer to provide a young Yazidi to rape. It isn't that easy to escape the swamp of one's humanity.

In ISIS territory, a man can be sentenced to death for smoking a cigarette, a woman for appearing in public with her head uncovered. But a killer clothed in Islamic purity doesn't fear getting his head cut off when he pays to see a prostitute or robs a house.

After several hours of testimony, Sharmin needs a break, and so do we. We leave the trailer to stretch our legs. As usual, I distance myself from the group to think this over.

For ISIS, the genocide of the Yazidis is by no means a gratuitous gesture. On the contrary, it is totally purposeful. "Useless" people—that is, the men who refuse to convert to Islamist ideology and those who are too old—are shot sooner or later. The very elderly too. Babies, Yazidi newborns, are kidnapped to be raised and trained as fighters. Young boys are turned into apprentice terrorists, providing ISIS with the means to fulfill its long-term objective: an international company of suicide terrorists without borders. A young Yazidi man, back from the camps, recalls what a guard said: "All of us are going to die, but you're young; you're the lion cubs of the caliphate. Later on, you'll become the fighters of the Islamic State." The girls who have been raped, beaten, sold, prostituted bring in money and provide sexual pleasure. They sometimes become wives, fighters, or potential suicide terrorists.

More and more, ISIS strikes me as a practice whose objective is clear: imposing its own Islamist ideology by every means possible on "its" territory, then beyond. The massacre of the Yazidis is genocide without a doubt, but genocide serving the ultimate goal of the Islamic State. Nevertheless, I wonder whether ISIS views the Yazidis purely from a regional perspective, or is its long-term strategy to have them participate in its expansion, by forcing them to commit terrorist acts outside Iraq and Syria? The future will tell.

This second hypothesis seems to be the more likely one. The bombings of Raqqa and Fallujah have altered the situation. We're getting more and more accounts by Yazidis who have recently escaped from those cities. According to them, certain ISIS men shave off their beards, on orders from the hierarchy, and make it known that they intend to melt into the floods of refugees. Some of them want to be "active" in Europe.

We return to Sharmin's interview. Just when we think we've gotten to the depths of the horrors, there is worse to come. She was sold again and was kept for a long time. Her new owner, a young bearded man of military bearing, kept her prisoner for eight months. Something in her voice, when she describes this man, catches my attention: she seems less resentful, less filled with pent-up hatred. I decide to press further:

"And your new master, how did he treat you? Did he also prostitute you for money?"

"No. He said to me: 'I won't hurt you if you do everything I tell you to.'" That little phrase makes me shudder. What was the price of no longer being considered a slave, bound and sold, night after night?

THE SUICIDE BOMBERS' GARAGE

After a long pause, we return to the interview. Sharmin looks tired. So do we. Everyone in the trailer is exhausted, physically and emotionally. We could break off and continue later, but the young woman refuses. She wants to speak now. She has something important to say. Yet she still hesitates. Her eyes dart everywhere, on the alert for a hidden enemy. Several times she starts, blurts out a few words. Then all of a sudden, she gags, looks off in the distance, then looks back at us, eyes sweeping left and right. With each attempt, there is a sensation of urgency. She's afraid she won't be able to say it but also afraid she will. She knows it's now or never, that by tomorrow she'll have had enough time to reflect and change her mind. She knows this is the point of no return. She's torn.

She finally mumbles a few words, a vague confession: "In order to stop being prostituted, I had to work in a terrorist 'workshop.'" We look at each other, uncomprehending. Her words are confused; she doesn't remember the place exactly.

She mentions an apartment, an office, an apartment again, and finally a garage. It's hard to understand what she's saying. She mixes up the locations where she was held prisoner, seems no longer able to situate the suffering she has endured. Mixing up the places is sometimes a sign of the difficulty of saying what really happened. The memory reawakens a pain so intense it's paralyzing.

Through our investigations in Eastern Europe, particularly in Romania and Moldova, Valy and I have gotten used to this kind of confusion. Valy remembers a Romanian village where a number of Jews were shot. We had discovered this Holocaust site while reporting on the deportation of Roma by Antonescu's men.[13] In fact, it happened that the same places were used for killing the Roma and the Jews. The more people we questioned, some of them sitting on a makeshift bench by the side of a road and others minding a cow in some green field, the more muddled the stories and the places where they'd occurred became. The mass grave we were searching for seemed to move from place to place depending on who was talking.

When witnesses fail to retrieve the memory of the precise spot where a crime occurred, when the location varies widely from one account to another, we know that this apparent confusion hides the most sordid of events, a crime that has become a nonplace, a nonevent. Finally, an old man cleared it up. He was present in the village at the time. A

---

13 Marshall Ion Antonescu led Romania during the Second World War and was complicit in the Nazi genocide of the Jews.

Romanian policeman who worked in a small train station would stop the trains carrying the Jews being deported, order the families who looked wealthy to get off, rob them, rape the women, and then shoot them before throwing them into a mass grave. It was inconceivably horrible.

For her part, Sharmin wants to speak, but something is still holding her back. She doesn't dare tell us the whole truth. She's camouflaging and rearranging the reality that she has lived—involuntarily, I believe. In this white trailer in alley D of the camp at Kadia, our legs have grown stiff from sitting so long, so we take time out for a breather. Then Zaher calmly approaches Sharmin. He speaks to her, one Yazidi to another, in a low voice, reassures her, and asks her questions. Brow furrowed, eyes downcast, gaze fixed on the ground, the young woman seems to reflect in silence. Abruptly, the dam breaks and she reveals the secret that has been stifling her, an ISIS secret, a "state secret."

On a number of occasions, her new master, Abu D., took her to a large garage, painted red on the outside—not unusual in this neighborhood of Mosul that had many of them—near the large mosque. Sharmin had no idea what awaited her. She was only too grateful that she was no longer being sold for the use of ISIS troops. Even if she had understood the world into which her owner was preparing to throw her, how could she have refused, when he was promising that she would no longer be prostituted?

Her jumbled words gave way to a detailed description. "From the outside, it was a hangar just like the others, with large sliding doors and the inscription GARAGE in capital letters." They would go there by car, a different one each day, a detail that intrigues me. Shamin's jailer moved around without bodyguards or escorts and switched vehicles. By all appearances, he was an important man who did his best to avoid notice by American drones.

Every morning before leaving for the garage, Abu D. would put on an explosive belt and force Sharmin to do the same. During her eight months in captivity, all day, every day, she wore that engine of death on her bruised body.

In front of us, seemingly unembarrassed, she repeats her daily routine, showing us how she used to adjust the belt around her waist. And her master never tired of foretelling her destiny as a forced suicide killer: "Someday, you'll blow yourself up."

In the garage, dozens of cars, white Toyotas, were aligned. Underneath them, fifteen or so workers busied themselves, torch in hand, cutting out a square of metal to install a circular bomb before resoldering the missing piece into place. Their work was painstaking: the operation had to be almost invisible, so that, in case it was checked with a mirror underneath at a checkpoint, the car would not be stopped. These workers, according to Sharmin, were between thirty and fifty years old. Two teams of fifteen people each took turns transforming the cars into killing machines.

We're astounded. We listen in total silence, immobile, lest the slightest movement by one of us disturb Sharmin's concentration and interrupt her story. The two teams of fifteen men, all from Mosul, according to her, kept up the activity in the garage nonstop. They would enter discreetly by a back door to avoid drawing the attention of neighbors on the street with any suspicious comings and goings as the two teams relieved each other.

Sharmin recalls one face in particular, a certain Abu I. On orders from Sharmin's owner, he didn't "repair" the cars but rather occupied a small office at the back of the garage on the right, where a phone was plugged in. He was in charge of managing the suicide candidates.

"How many people volunteered each day?" I ventured to ask.

"Between ten and twenty," she replied calmly.

"And what nationality were they?"

"Iraqis from Mosul, Syrians, Chechens, and Saudis."

"Were there any Europeans?"

"No."

The candidates were received in the garage by the same Abu I., who tested them and "selected" them. Like a job interview, but one in which the successful candidates would work for only one day, a contract with death, their own and that of other people. The mission—to kill and die as an assassin. On the day of the suicide attack, Abu D. would call them in and install them at the wheel of a car that had been "prepared" by the garage's teams. The drivers were to wear ordinary clothes. Sharmin is unable to say how many cars she saw leaving, but it was a lot, truly a lot. Sometimes one or two a day.

Turning an ordinary garage, one of many in a neighborhood full of car-repair shops, into a launching center for cars crammed with explosives . . . a clever idea. What could be more banal in a big city like Mosul than cars entering and leaving a garage?

Sharmin explains that the suicide drivers often left in convoys of two or three cars. They drove the cars themselves to the destination. Ever since, I think of the Mosul garage every time I hear the news of the day, see the terrible images, hear the journalists say, "Two suicide cars exploded in front of a hotel/police station/school, causing many deaths and an unknown number of injuries." Macabre as it is, the procedure is used so often it has lost its novelty. Never would I have imagined finding myself face to face, without having sought it, with a young forced slave of this terrorist factory.

Valy helps the young woman draw the garage on a large sheet of white paper. She goes on to explain the day-to-day workings of the suicide drivers' garage. The cars were equipped with metal plaques which, ironically, protected the driver from being shot head-on. The future martyrs were given a road map as well as the route to follow and the target to hit. It wasn't enough simply to prepare the vehicles; the garage owner also had to make sure that the suicide attackers fulfilled their goal. Sharmin remembers that he got calls regularly. He wasn't the one who decided to send young people to their deaths; he got orders over the phone.

I'm used to hearing accounts of murders and atrocities. I've learned to stay calm in all circumstances, at least on the surface, but I admit that these revelations, which I was in no way prepared for, shook me. When an interview takes a turn that surprises me, I decide not to worry, or rather to pretend not to worry about anything other than the issues of a practical nature encountered by criminals in the act of committing their crimes.

I remember interviewing a young Ukrainian woman who, as a child, had found out that a number of Jews on the farm where she was living had been killed by her parents at night. To maintain my stoic composure, I asked her, "It must have been upsetting having all those dead Jews in your house in the morning?" She put on her green rubber boots and a heavy jacket to protect her from the cold and invited me to follow her: "Come, I'll show you." She led me past a sign marking the end of the village, and, leaving the road, led me to eighteen little common graves. "I transported the bodies myself in my wheelbarrow."

I interrupt Sharmin with a seemingly naïve question: "Road maps? Of Syria, of Iraq? It's hard to find them in shops!" Her answer, tragic though it is, makes me smile. "Yes, that's true. There aren't very many. They made photocopies." So a photocopier had been installed in the garage to meet the demand for road maps for the deadly enterprise.

Following up on my interest in the practical dimensions of the operation, Valy asks for specifics concerning the detonator of the explosives. On the white sheet of paper, Sharmin reproduces a life-size version of the remote control given to the suicide attackers: "They were metal, except for the button. They made them in the garage." Everything was custom-made, then, except for the button. Just like at the Belzec extermination camp, set up by the Germans in eastern Poland. The first gas chamber had been built by a village carpenter whom I'd been able to question at his home. In the most natural way in the world, he explained how he had made the doors: two wooden planks with sand in the middle so that the Jews waiting outside wouldn't hear the people dying inside. I still see him, sitting on a chair, repeating the gestures of the craftsman he had been when he constructed the machinery of death. I was familiar with the craftsmanship of death, Nazi-style. But the criminal methodology of ISIS in the twenty-first century, combining the archaic and the modern, professionalism and craftsmanship, is an astonishing example of human ingenuity in the service of mass murder.

In the suicide attackers' garage, they also made bombs with cans and gas canisters that were filled with an explosive product and then resoldered and connected to a telephone. These bombs were stocked in two closed rooms adjacent to the garage. Sharmin is still drawing. The bombs installed in the vehicles were round and had holes in the center.

One day, Sharmin saw twenty cars leave at the same time. I ask her about the morale of the suicide bombers' state of mind. Were they sure of themselves? Did they have a moment of hesitation before driving to their death? Not surprisingly, she explains that the drug they were given took away their fear. "It was like flour." Abu D. didn't keep the drug in the garage but under lock and key in his house. At the moment of the terrorists' departure, he was present. He gave them the drug and showed them on the map the place each was supposed to target.

We're so staggered by Sharmin's testimony that we forget to ask her what her exact role was in the garage. She doesn't volunteer this information. Perhaps talking about it is too difficult for her. Perhaps also, during this session, our expressions gave away how surprised and disturbed we were. Maybe Sharmin felt she couldn't go any further, that we couldn't take any more. Witnesses to murder never stop measuring, thinking through what their listeners can bear. As for us, it would take us weeks to fully digest these revelations.

In the darkness of my room, I reflect on Sharmin's testimony. So the men of ISIS break their prisoners the way people uproot trees, taking them to the breaking point. Then sometimes they suddenly offer to stop the torture on the condition that the victim become an active link in the terrorist chain. So how do they choose the prisoners who'll give in to this blackmail, will agree to accept this false "privileged" status in order to survive? Abu D. felt no affection for Sharmin. The fact that every morning he forced her to attach a belt of explosives around her waist is telling: at all times, he maintained the power of life or death over her. He couldn't set off Sharmin's belt himself,[14] but the instructions were clear: if captured, they were supposed to blow themselves up. Would the young woman have done it? Broken by the long months of forced prostitution, Sharmin was a person living in abeyance.

I'm inclined to think that Sharmin's story is far from an isolated case and that it reveals the treatment ISIS reserves for certain long-term Yazidi captives—eighteen months in Sharmin's case. After such an extended period, hostages have been crushed. Abuse has overwhelmed their resistance and their will to preserve their identity. They're ready to accept almost anything that will make the pain stop. They're ready to stop thinking and to act robotically like the men of ISIS.

---

14 A detonator, connected to the belt by a wire, has to be activated to set off an explosion.

The Islamic State doesn't have a monopoly on this method. Recently, the press revealed that a young girl kidnapped by Boko Haram had blown herself up on a target. Was this a voluntary act? Had her suffering induced her to accept her torturer's ideology in order to put an end to her pain? Did they force her? There may be no clear answer to this question. Daily humiliation and physical and mental torture obliterate prisoners' freedom, making it impossible for them to think for themselves. Denied as individuals, they may see death as benign or even attractive in comparison.

Beyond the strategic aspect, which once again demonstrates the Islamic State's nuanced understanding of human nature, in my opinion this reveals the three dimensions of ISIS: fundamentalist, to be sure, but also militarist and terrorist. When a suicide attacker blows himself up, the target is often tactical. The use of violence by ISIS is a military act similar to the kamikaze attacks by the Japanese pilots who crashed into American ships. The purpose is to weaken the enemy's defenses physically to gain territory. But human and material damage isn't the only objective. ISIS is also a terrorist enterprise. I remember an attack on Rehov Ben Yehuda, a pedestrian street in Jerusalem, where three different attackers blew themselves up, one by one. In the following months, stores closed one after the other. The Islamist suicide attacker kills like a military man and spreads terror at the same time. As Frédéric Encel says, a terrorist terrorizes. Last, the act has a religious basis, since the Islamist suicide attacker is confident that he'll be handsomely rewarded in heaven, that he'll be a martyr.

If ISIS is motivated solely by religious considerations, as its leaders claim, why offer slaves the kind of paradise reserved for martyrs, why allow them the prospect of the same rewards as those earned by jihadists who subscribe to the Islamist ideology? An entity conveniently garbed in the cloak of a radical religion that authorizes abuses of every sort, the Islamic State is nonetheless possessed of realism when it comes to military and terrorist matters: it is sometimes better to sacrifice a slave than one of their own.

After the interview, in the streets of the camp, off-camera, without recording equipment, Valy brings me a telephone. On the screen is the face of a young man with wavy black hair, wearing a sand-colored outfit. He's posing, standing upright for the photo. "This is Abu D., the owner of the suicide bombers' garage!" he exclaims. Then he explains at length what he is going to do:

"I'll have my revenge!" He's angry. He's talking fast, excitedly.

Valy's family history is rife with tragedies. He wasn't yet born in 1942 when the Romanian military police, with the complicity of the mayor, entered his village of Garla Mare. They rounded up all the Roma families in the municipal building and stripped them of their possessions before loading them onto a train. In the camps where they were transported, they died of poverty and sickness or the beatings of the Romanians and the Ukrainians who were holding them captive. The girls were raped in view of their families, often by neighbors of the camps, and the bodies were piled up in an enormous mass grave.

Valy doesn't know who was responsible for the massacre of his family and the elimination of a part of his roots.

Sharmin's testimony sickens him. Unable to help his own people and still feeling bitter frustration seventy years after the fact, he has made it his mission to aid this martyred people whose experience is so similar to his own. "We must tell the world what is happening here—right now!"

As for me, the grandson of Claudius Desbois, deported to Camp 325, I'm having trouble holding back my tears. Zaher, a member of this people that ISIS is persecuting, is standing nearby and seems moved, too. His smile is icy.

Suddenly, a verse of the Bible comes to me: "And if a man prevail against him that is alone, two shall withstand him; and a threefold cord is not quickly broken." We are three intertwined cords, but also three sons, three scions bearing memories of those who have been deported, scorned, humiliated, sometimes murdered. Tonight, under this beautiful Iraqi sky, I turn to Him in whom I believe. I am standing, tired, silent before God, a few kilometers from ISIS territory, a few steps from hell. And I say in defiance, "Look!"

Excerpt from the Interview with Sharmin

Were the bombs all alike, or were there different kinds?
There were several types of bombs: they made them out of bottles and tomato-juice cans.

How did they make the bombs out of cans?
They would put the product into the cans; then they ran a wire in the hole.

How many cans were tied together?
Two, next to each other.

Was the bomb remote-controlled by a telephone?
Yes, by a telephone. They would take the wire from the cans and plug it into the phone.

To set off the bomb, they would call the number of the telephone, right?
Yes, that's right.

How old were the people who came to work?
They were adults. Thirty-one years old, fifty, sixty, and older.

Which bomb was more powerful, the bottle or the can?
The bottle.

What did they blow up the cans with?
They would put them in the ground.

Did Abu D.'s boss phone regularly?
He'd contact him every two or three days. He was the one who told him where he should plant the bombs.

Would Abu D. go away alone or with his team of fifteen people?
He'd go off alone.

Did he plant the bombs? Was he proud of doing that?
Yes, he would also put the explosives in the cars.

Ah, yes! Where did he put the explosives? In the car?
He was the one who made the explosives. He would solder the bombs under the car and a metal plaque in the front of the car to protect it from bullets.

Did someone drive the car to blow it up?
Yes.

How many cars were there?
Lots. Maybe a hundred.

Who found the suicide attackers? Was it Abu D. who chose them?
No, they volunteered. Lots of them came from Syria. Many had lost their family.

Did they come directly to the garage? Or did they phone?
No, they came to the garage to register. It was Abu I. who wrote the names in the register.

Were there any people who came to be suicide attackers and were turned down?
No, all the people who came wanting to be suicide attackers were registered.

In your opinion, how many people came every day?
About ten a day.

Is that why they needed a lot of cars?
Yes.

Did people carry out suicide attacks alone or in pairs?
They would go out several at a time but not in the same car.

How many cars would go out together?
Sometimes three or four cars would go out at the same time.

Were they always the same cars?
Yes, always white Toyotas.

Were the bombs they soldered under the cars made from cans or bottles?
No, they were round bombs.

Were those bombs made in the garage or did they come in crates?
He was the one who made them. The bombs were round and in the middle there was a hole and he covered it with cloth.

And when the bomb was placed under the car, how did they set it off?
There was a wire with a metal lever, with a plastic button. The lever was made in the garage too. They made everything in the garage.

Was Abu D. proud to do all that?
Yes. He would show me videos of suicide attackers who blew themselves up. He also said to me, "I am going to put you into a car so you blow yourself up on some Yazidis."

Did he make you wear an explosives belt?
Yes, every time I went out.

When you went out in public, did he forbid you to tell people that you were a Yazidi?
Yes, he told me to pretend I was a fighter.

Did he really want you to blow yourself up?
Whatever he told me, I said yes. But I wanted to run away. I tried three times, but they stopped me. Then he brought me back to his place.

In his house?
Yes, after two months in the garage, he took me into his house. I stayed at his house for eight months.

Did he want to have children with you?
Yes. He thought I would never leave.

How were you able not to get pregnant?
I had taken pills and an injection to avoid getting pregnant.

In the hospital?
No, at the house. It was his wife who gave me the injection.

Was his wife nice?
No, she was always mean. She treated me like a *khadima*, a servant.

And when you were in the garage, did he let you stay in a corner and do nothing, or did he make you work?
He made me work. I transported bottles.

How many bottles were there in the garage?
Lots. A room filled with bottles. And another room for the cans. And still another one for the bombs for the suicide attackers.

When they were preparing a suicide attacker, did they put him in a car? What did they do? Did they phone the suicide attacker?
Abu D. was in charge. He was the one who would phone the person.

How many suicide attackers would leave every day?
Once I saw twenty of them go out to blow themselves up.

But when they went out, was it in a convoy or alone?
Each suicide bomber went out alone.

Did they pray before they left?
Yes, they had a little Koran with them.

Did they wear any special clothes? An ISIS uniform?
No, they wore civilian clothes. But they wore beards.

Were there any women among the suicide attackers?
No, there were no women.

How old was the youngest suicide killer you saw leaving to blow himself up?
The youngest one was fifteen years old.

SINJAR LIBERATED

An immense field of gravel, a long city in ruins. Under the leaden sky, the main street is windswept, and the dust from the rubble churns in the grayish air. Only the electric poles remain standing on both sides of the deserted street, mute witnesses to what the city once was. Broken wires hang and swing. This is the first time I'm crossing a ghost city so recently ravaged.

Sinjar, which we've heard so much about. Sinjar, liberated at last. But destroyed.

So many Yazidis have told us about Sinjar, their capital, their emblematic city, their mountain, their holy place, their cradle, their pride, the seat of their identity.

Shielded by the armored car whose doors are so heavy I to have to strain every time I open them, I look out at the unreal scene, absolutely desolate, something out of a Hollywood movie. Reality is stranger than fiction.

We had to drive around Mount Sinjar on the Iraqi side to

get here. We made it, not without difficulty. Danger lurks. The guards are heavily armed, leery about being so close to the front line. We passed through several Sunni villages, ghost towns also, their houses doorless, windowless, empty.

And we've finally arrived. In Sinjar, or at least what's left of it.

Before our astonished eyes, here is the result of a cursed marriage between blood-soaked ideological radicalism haloed in religious imagery, the war waged in its name, and the genocide justified by its precepts. I can hardly believe that liberated Sinjar almost doesn't exist anymore, that it's nothing but what I see.

Two Peshmerga soldiers guard the entrance to the city. What an incongruous image—they're sitting at the side of the tar-covered road on a large, colorful sofa, a piece of living-room furniture that looks quite comfortable set directly on the ground. Behind them, behind the sofa, is rubble. And that's all.

Killing a people isn't just killing its members; it's also eradicating its memory, its geography, making sure that they'll never return. ISIS raped Sinjar. The silence surrounding it is deafening and soul-wrenching.

Preceding our car is a military vehicle with a masked man standing behind an improvised metal shield, leaning on his weapon of war. He scans the horizon watchfully. Other military vehicles follow, driven by heavily armed Yazidis bent on revenge. Many have joined the Peshmergas. They want want to regain possession of what used to be their territory and to restore their honor.

I have the strange sensation of being alive in the midst of nothingness invaded by death—of men and their structures—going down streets that no longer lead anywhere. I don't know where to look. Our team doesn't speak. We barely communicate by gestures, sounds, murmurs, and broken syllables. We're assailed, buried, gradually walled in by the battered landscape that stretches as far as the eye can see. The consequences of explosions and combat and violence are everywhere. Not a single store is left standing. Yet here and there is a sign, a poster, a relic of daily life long past. One of the signs that avoided the wreck, a triangular remnant of the past, warns: WATCH FOR CHILDREN CROSSING THE STREET.

The irony prompts a bitter smile. Farther on, as if a crude reminder of the uselessness of this warning, a blue-and-white baby seat floats on the blackened remains of a house with blown-out doors. We move along through the debris of a modern world that has been crumpled, destroyed by terrorism and bombed by its liberators.

On the ruins of a garage and a bakery, I notice identical hand-painted inscriptions. The whole village is dotted with the same words. "It's in Arabic, the ISIS slogan," explains Zaher. The Islamic State has apparently etched its presence everywhere. Both inside and outside, the walls that are still standing bear drawings of the ISIS flag, the signature of their occupation.

"There was no way other than bombing them to drive them out," a Peshmerga whispers sadly upon seeing our appalled expressions. I know he's telling the truth. It was the same with the Nazis in Germany. Without the massive bombardment of German cities flying their swastika-emblazoned red flags, would Hitler have lost the war?

We get out of the cars. We walk carefully, following the footsteps of the guards, in case a mine might be slumbering in the rubble. The head of the team warned us: "Don't pick up anything, not even a stone or a child's toy. Anything could be a mine. We haven't had time to clean up the whole city, and they've planted them everywhere."

A leveled Orthodox church, of which almost nothing still stands—in any case, nothing to remind us that it was a Christian monument—is exposing its innards. Some Yazidis have hung a meager little wooden cross on one of the remaining walls. I feel nothing. My spirit is in too much pain to think, but my eyes seem suddenly unable to obey my will, and they weep. I feel obligated to justify myself to my team—it must be some sort of allergy. Sometimes, while listening to the accounts of the survivors of genocide, the body reacts despite the barricades built by the rational part of the brain that is indispensable for the investigation. The wind keeps swirling the dust that lands on our skin, penetrating everywhere, saturating the atmosphere with tangible proof of the void. We're breathing the end of a world.

"Do you want to see one of the ISIS tunnels?" a Yazidi asks suddenly. He invites us to follow him to a large building. The doors resists; it seems locked. He gestures to us to move away, in case the house is booby-trapped, and armed guards swarm in through the broken windows to knock down the door.

We enter in turn. I'm surprised at what I see. The interior no longer looks fit for habitation. The house is full of carefully arranged sandbags piled up to the ceiling, between which the guards pick their way to the entrance of the tunnel. We look at each other in silence. The tunnel was dug in such a way that not a single bag of sand left the house—an excavation invisible from above, from the drones patrolling the sky. I remain fearful, mistrustful. I'm afraid the tunnel is mined. Only Oscar, the photographer, rushes into it, camera in hand. I take a look around. A small Koran is resting in a corner, abandoned in the sand.

Rather than pass through the tunnel, I want to find its exit. Someone shows me where the emir of Sinjar's house is. We have to walk a little. The building partially withstood the bombing. This house impresses me. As if the emir had left just a short while ago, there are some rolls on a plate, waiting to be eaten. In the entryway, on the wall to the left, there are large letters in Arabic writing. Zaher translates: "It's the name of the emir." "Over a meter long," I hear myself murmur. "The emir's radical Islam doesn't seem to have burdened him with humility."

Another detail catches my eye: leaning against a wall in the large room are two cardboard signs, similarly emblazoned with Arabic words. "That's to teach people who don't know the prayers how to pray," says Zaher. "All the details of praying are written here, along with the gestures to make." What to make of this? Did the emir of Sinjar, like so many others, have female Yazidi slaves who'd been converted by force and were unable to pray without the help of these signs? If that's the case, where were they now? Or were these inscriptions intended for use by Westerners who'd come to join the ranks of ISIS? Or for children? I'll never know.

I go a little farther, into what used to be his hideout. The emir's room is unusual. He slept in a narrow space, here too surrounded by sandbags piled up to the ceiling. A bunker. Dug into the ground this way, he probably felt protected from bullets and bombardments, and in case of attack, the tunnel would provide an escape route.

Later on, we would hear much testimony about the daily lives of the leaders of the Islamic State. The testimony makes clear that the emirs (or the *walis*), so quick to sow death and to order a good number of young people, often from far away, to die as martyrs, found ways to guarantee themselves a quick death. Although he had no doubt sent many young suicide bombers to blow themselves up in various strategic places, the emir of Sinjar had deployed an elaborate security system to protect his own life. Much later, a young Yazidi woman would tell us that the emir of Anbach never went out with his face uncovered. Furthermore, he was connected by walkie-talkie with a whole network for advance warning about the sound of drones or planes in the area. If ISIS authorities wear explosive belts, it's so they can be used in case of capture: "If caught, I will not be taken prisoner. I'll blow myself up."

Five o'clock in the afternoon. Children scatter, apparently from a small improvised school, and they run through the ruins, returning to whatever remains of their homes. One of the Peshmerga accompanying us for security reasons suddenly loses his composure in a moment of weakness. He relates in an emotional tone: "A woman came to see me. They had decapitated her baby. . . ." He's crying under his hood, unable to say any more, overwhelmed by the memory of that woman who had been able to keep one of her baby's earrings. We are all extremely moved. This man who has been protecting us since this morning, standing up on his vehicle, his face covered, is now crying under his hood. He apologizes and resumes his military stance.

"Let's go see the central administrative building of Sinjar," I say in a loud voice. Valy agrees; Zaher is surprised. "Administrative center? It no longer exists." I insist. We climb over the rubble and jump on cinder blocks until we reach the entrance, which now looks out on nothing. "It's there," remarks Zaher, "next to the exercise room." I look. Nothing remains of the exercise room except the entrance. Zaher, a Yazidi, speaks of various sites in Sinjar as if their life still flowed in his veins. The building, lacking its façade, is enormous. The belly of the genocide.

This is where large numbers of Yazidis from Sinjar and the nearby villages, men, women, and children, had been herded together. The girls were locked in the upper stories; down below were the mothers. I look over the remains of this floor, its windows closed off with bars, from which the girls had to watch their men leaving, never to return.

Today, there are no more screams, no more violence, just gusts of wind. The administrative building gapes open, exposed to the four winds, no doubt leveled in the bombing. Valy and Zaher have climbed with difficulty onto the platform of the ground floor; they scrounge around in the debris, get up, and show me ID cards of Yazidis deceased before the war. They found them on the ground, which is strewn with documents of all sorts. This was the local administration headquarters, the first step in the massacre, like the city halls in Romania for the Roma, like the police stations in France for the Jews. These walls, which once represented order and authority, a well-established system for administering the lives of the population, had been transformed into triage centers. The invaders decided who would live, who would be enslaved, who would die.

I'm finally discovering the places the surviving Yazidi refugees have been describing in their testimony in the camps. Valy carefully records the GPS coordinates of the site. Who knows whether tomorrow there will remain a single cement panel, a trace? In a flash, I remember something. I turn on my computer to verify the information that's coming back to me. Avine was locked up not far from here, in the Solakh Institute. I ask Valy to locate the area on the map. In a few seconds, he finds it. I ask the Peshmerga, "Has Solakh been liberated?" A large smile lights up the face that has been chiseled by the sun: "Yes, Solakh is free." We pile into the cars to go there.

A cement building, immense, beige, an empty courtyard. It's very different from what I'd imagined. The walls are intact, rising insolently in this ravaged countryside. The roof has been caved in by bombs. Above the main floor of the empty building is a single story. Young girls upstairs, "mothers" below. Something Avine said pops into my mind: "My mother was psychologically fragile. I tried to hide her behind a desk so they wouldn't take her away. They found her and hit her with cables." I feel a pang in my heart. That happened here, where I'm now walking. This is where Avine saw her mother for the last time. We decide to call her: she has obtained refugee status in Germany.

I climb over the rubble. I want to enter, to walk in the places where ISIS sowed death, to follow the steps of the slaves in this place of suffering where selection and separation of the victims were done. The institute is huge; I see now why ISIS requisitioned it to lock up prisoners. I hadn't pictured a building so large. There was room in it for many, many people. It's also entirely cut off from the rest of the city.

Life has been sucked out of the area. Papers with the institute letterhead fly around the ground, an odd remnant of the bureaucratic order of the past in the midst of the current chaos. I remember the accounts of women locked up within these walls, the mothers and the young girls, packed in together, terrified, trying in vain to avoid being selected. Some of them simply stand in stony silence, displaying a dignity that hides their inner torment. Others feel completely defenseless, silently weeping or crying openly. The ISIS men, register in hand and weapons or whips poised, sort through them, over and over again. The young mothers cling tightly to their babies, trying to reassure them.

Solakh was the second place where Avine was incarcerated. From there she and the others were sent to Mosul, then to Tal Afar, prey to the gratuitous violence of their guards and their neighbors. Little by little, they were transformed into subjects of ISIS, dressed in the black *niqabs*, gloves, socks, and shoes that constituted their official attire, buried alive in Islamist ideology and authorized sadism.

I look up. A nervous silence draws me out of my thoughts. The guards suddenly tense up. Zaher points to the horizon. He explains to Valy, "You see them over there, that's ISIS. You see their cars going by?" Yes, we see on the other side of the no-man's-land, on their side, a zone outside of the law. Even though they're so close, I'm not afraid. I can't explain why. I'm driven by some strange necessity that propels me from one room to the other. I walk through the rooms, I look them all over, prod my memory, summon forth the testimony in an attempt to reconstruct the criminal process that unfolded in this place.

The institute in Solakh is one of the many ISIS crime scenes. "How did the older women get out?" I asked. The expressions of the Yazidis accompanying us darken. They gesture toward the back of the institute. "There," they reply, looking sad. Eighty-four older people apparently were killed, along with a group of fifteen-year-olds, and thrown into a pool behind the building, a little closer to the front.

Before I know it, my legs are carrying me out of the institute, right up to said pool. The bodyguards surround us, their eyes riveted on the ISIS positions. The empty pool is now covered with vegetation, but it isn't dense enough to hide the white traditional garments, the belts of a yellowish orange, the clothing of older women. It doesn't take long to make out human remains. My eyes fix on a skull with a hole in it. I think with sadness of Avine, who hoped her mother was being held captive somewhere, still alive. She must be here still, under our gaze, one body among the tangled piles of women's bodies, discarded haphazardly.

ISIS is coldly pragmatic when it comes to mass killing. People who are of no use to them are immediately murdered. Usefulness is the condition for survival of a prisoner.

The guards pull me out of my reflections. Two ISIS mortars have just fallen not very far away. We have to leave.

Absorbed by the questions this mass grave raises, I've heard nothing and haven't noticed the impact of the shells. Smoke is rising in the sky. Valy, aware of the risk, is preparing the vehicles to get us away from the front line.

On the way back, I notice that there are bodies all around the wadi. It's a horrifying spectacle: hair, human bones gnawed by dogs, children's clothes, prayer beads in a dried-up river bed, Wadi Zelleli. "Why were so many people killed here?" wonders Valy. The men accompanying us explain that some Yazidis fled toward Mount Sinjar following the course of the river. Valy notes the GPS coordinates of the massacre site, which the photographer preserves for posterity. They got caught by ISIS. "About fifty people were shot." Farther on, still along the river, there are small mass graves. The men of ISIS hunted the Yazidis down like animals. They weren't simply trying to remove them from their territory; they wanted them to die.

The "liberated" territory here is dotted with burial grounds. A Yazidi Peshmerga, approaching one of them, points out a brown garment on the ground, some piles of bones, eyeglasses, prayer beads: "This is my uncle," he murmurs. I look at him. Behind his glasses, his eyes are unmoving. He has a thick mustache. I look at the uncle, murdered, the prayer beads. My heart aches.

EPILOGUE

May 2016—Paris

It's now time to make a provisional report. We're going to have to come back to gather more evidence of this genocide that has been going on for two years, despite the bombing. Last summer, I set out, loaded with questions, to meet Yazidis who were victims of Islamist ideology. I was expecting to meet a people murdered for ideological religious reasons, knowing full well that totalitarian ideology is never the sole motivation for genocide.

From the very first day, the meetings with Yazidis were full of surprises. I found a people still standing, dignified, unbowed, and smiling despite its gaping wounds. Throughout their testimony, little by little, the Machiavellian cunning that the Islamic State has been exercising against them is becoming clear.

From the beginning to the "end" of the investigation, I couldn't help but notice the contradictions between the ideological purity claimed by ISIS and their barbaric acts against men, women, and children. Today, I'm convinced of it: the Yazidis aren't being persecuted simply because they're considered to be heretics. They're being persecuted because it is profitable for ISIS.

Their genocide seems to me to be above all utilitarian. They represent a considerable pool of resources: first of all, they're heaven-sent financially, for they're immediately robbed upon their arrest but then also sold and resold. The slave trade organized by ISIS is highly lucrative. Slavery, the leaders of ISIS say, is authorized by Islamist ideology. Enslaving Yazidis gives free rein to everyone, from the lowliest combatant to the highest authority, to exercise their sadistic impulses. This sadism isn't considered a fault, for the Islam practiced by ISIS authorizes the enslavement and the rape of young women and girls. Legalized sexual cruelty crosses all strata of the caliphate. As for children, they're trained in order to swell the ranks of the Islamic State as future combatants, terrorists, and kamikaze-like suicide bombers.

On a deeper level, the caliphate offers a position of superiority to those who enter the territory controlled by men and women who adhere to "absolute truth." This superiority expresses itself in the form of the cruelest acts toward the local populations who submit only when coerced. Recently, a young Yazidi woman told us that the man who had bought her was a member of the religious police in Deir ez-Zor. He would walk through the markets checking to make sure no parts of women's bodies were visible. If a single glove had been left at home, the guilty party risked prison and beatings.

The caliphate is also a slaveholding regime, though rarely denounced as such. Every ISIS fighter who buys one or more female Yazidi slaves automatically gains enhanced status. At his home or in a hotel, he's the sole possessor of a girl upon whom he can exercise all manner of sadistic violence, all in the name of the absolute truth to which he thinks he professes. The caliphate offers absolute superiority to its adherents by decreeing a people, the Yazidis, to be below them. The Yazidis are to ISIS what the populations considered inferior were to the Nazis. There is no such thing as a race of supermen. On the other hand, total dominance over a people who have been subjugated or eliminated ensures the illusion of superiority within the human race. It confers the impression of being a superhuman.

When it authorizes murder, slavery, and torture, the privilege of absolute power over a people in the name of God offers the dominant group a feeling of invincibility.

In addition, the genocide of the Yazidis by the Islamic State is unusual in that it applies to all parts of the territories under the control of ISIS. The Yazidis can be locked up not only in training camps, prisons, and schools but also within the families of the followers, sometimes in the privacy of their homes. One survivor told us that not only would her owner rape her in front of his wife but that the wife would hold her legs apart during the rape. The women and children of ISIS members often participate fully in the genocide. The topography of genocide thus permeates even the private lives of the fighters and the men in power. Certain Yazidi women who are servants of ISIS families are beaten by the fathers, the wives, and the children.

Ownership of Yazidi slaves is available to the men of ISIS irrespective of their position in the hierarchy. Lowly workers in the oil fields of Deir ez-Zor can purchase and enslave a girl and lock her up in their trailer. At the highest levels, the *walis* and the sheikhs can also acquire one slave or several that they can transform into mute companions. Genocidal activity isn't reserved for someone in authority or the guards of a camp. By purchasing a slave, everyone can enjoy the pleasures of absolute dominance right at home.

As of today, we've interviewed more than ninety people who've been freed from this genocidal slavery. Each one has been able to give us more than ten names of men and women of ISIS who committed unspeakable and innumerable crimes, convinced that their god authorized this violence because the same god has designated the Yazidis as *kuffar.*

The privilege of genocide can thus be acquired by every member of the Islamic State; absolute dominance over the Yazidis is the blackboard on which the men and women of the caliphate inscribe their religious superiority.

The Yazidis aren't the only ones inscribed on the scale of this hierarchy. Christians, Shiites, nonbelievers, and homosexuals also have their places. A system of dominance that confers at every moment the power of life or death is attractive, even in the twenty-first century. Attractive enough to be worth dying for.

But genocidal acts, unlike the genocidal speech publicized by the media and social networks, aren't crowned with the halo of purity. Little eight-year-old girls are raped, sometimes to the point of death. A young mother spoke with us for two hours without being able to look straight at us. Eyes riveted on the ground, surrounded by her two children, including the eight-year-old, she spoke on and on. All of a sudden, she asked her daughter to leave the tent. She related that one day they took the little girl away from her. When she returned, the mother tried to find out what had happened. Every time she asked a question, the girl passed out. The mother questioned older girls, who recounted the unspeakable events. The child had been stripped and raped by the guards. Valy couldn't bear the shock of that interview. I felt ashamed of the human race. That little girl who had been raped revealed all the inhumanity of the ideology of ISIS.

Young girls bought and sold, sometimes prostituted. The incessant body searches of Yazidi prisoners to strip them of everything they owned, including items that didn't always end up in the coffers of the caliphate. The murder of infidels, the public tortures of unimaginable cruelty—the Marquis de Sade's writings pale in comparison. Recently, the killers have started engaging the crowd in these crimes. Spectators were given weapons and fired. Gleefully.

There is no such thing as pure genocidal murder. The cloak of purity authorizes genocide but doesn't cover the murderers and their acts. They are slavers who worship the idol of their own selves. ISIS may pretend to justify its crimes, but whatever it says, it cannot ensure the purity of the killers. The commitment of some of them, whether voluntarily or by force, to become suicide attackers or shooters who are willing to die the way the Paris killers did would seem to lend credence to their belief in some sort of absolute truth. But the words of Yazidis who have escaped slavery reveal the hidden recesses of the men and women in black.

I cannot end this book without sharing a question that has been haunting me since the beginning of our research. Many nongovernmental, state, and UN organizations have justifiably criticized the genocidal actions of ISIS. But this genocide has one peculiarity: no one has been designated as the guilty party. The Yazidis genocide consists only of victims.

Neither Abu Bakr al-Baghdadi nor his *walis*—who are often eliminated by means of bullets or drone strikes, like Abu Waheeb earlier this month—nor those recently arrested in France, Belgium, and Turkey have been denounced and treated as the perpetrators of a genocide. I'm well aware that it's hard to personally implicate a young shooter from the streets of Paris or Brussels in this. But shouldn't Abu Bakr al-Baghdadi be named and accused of being the coordinator and organizer of the genocide of the Yazidis?

The weary voices of Yazidi girls, women, and grandmothers point to the guilty parties. The list of names spelled out by the survivors is long and involves men and women who are certainly for the most part Iraqis or Syrians, but also Moroccans, Tunisians, Algerians, Lebanese, Jordanians, Saudis, Libyans, Germans, French, Belgians, Norwegians, British, Australians, Canadians, Americans, Chinese . . .

If no member of ISIS were to be designated as an active agent responsible for the genocide of the Yazidis, the risk for mankind would be enormous. It would confer upon the whole military and terrorist enterprise the possibility of engaging in a utilitarian genocide without the agents of mass murder ever having to answer for this accusation.

Hitler too was able to confer a cloak of purity on the men who participated in the genocide of Jews, under the military pretext of the fight against Bolshevism. The genocide trials of Auschwitz guards, even seventy years later, ought to remind us that responsibility for genocide remains a personal one. Will we have to wait sixty-six years for a guard at the prison in Raqqa, where Yazidis were detained, to be hauled before a judge?

Once revealed publicly, the genocide of the Jews and Roma exposed the true face of the promise of Aryan purification. The voices of the Yazidi victims can also expose the dark underside of the discourse of purity proffered by the men and women who have allied themselves with Abu Bakr al-Baghdadi.

In Iraq, ISIS is eradicating a people—its members, its traditions, its memory, its places—and is honing a fearsome terrorist war machine that is well organized, strategic, and determined. The destructive ingenuity of ISIS must be recognized before it's too late for Lawin, Payman, Bahar, and Sharmin—but also for us.

The Islamic State is no more nor less than a factory for terrorists, which, thanks to the martyrdom of the Yazidis, reveals the formula for its expansion: sex, money, and power. The perfect storm. The three pillars of the Islamic State.

I am coming to the end of writing this book, which is a cry and a plea. It is the screams of men who have been shot dead, of women reduced to slavery, of children who have been indoctrinated—it is the plea of the Yazidis, broken and massacred by ISIS in the name of an insane warping of religion.

ACKNOWLEDGMENTS

Thanks:

To Zedo Hassan, investigator.
To Andrej Umansky, our legal advisor.
To Marco Gonzalez and Emmanuel Cortey, for their support.
To Rezan Khlil, Souhaib, Rangeen Shukry, Hama Khalaf,
Wilde Khalid Asmail, Sayd Murad, Avine, Kamal Saido,
Subhi Ahmad, without whom we could never have
entered the camps.
To Pauline Bonvalet, for her invaluable help.
To Howard Hoffen and Lily Safra, who believed in this fight.
To Lara Logan.